Reclaiming Your Soul

Wisdom from the Gospel of Luke

Daniel D. Schroeder

BeneVentura, LLC
PO Box 414
Hortonville, WI 54944

Copyright © 2015 by Daniel D. Schroeder

All rights reserved. No part of this book may be reproduced, stored in a retrieval system, or transmitted in any form or by any means, electronic, mechanical, including photocopying, recording, or otherwise, without the written permission of the copyright holder.

The Scripture quotations contained herein are from the New Revised Standard Version of the Bible, copyright © 1989 by the Division of Christian Education of the National Council of the Churches of Christ in the U.S.A., and are used by permission. All rights reserved.

First Edition, January 2015

Printed in the United States of America

ISBN   9780692353967

Cover design: Kristi Roekle

Reclaiming Your Soul

Wisdom from the Gospel of Luke

God will not take away a life; he will devise plans so as not to keep an outcast banished forever from his presence.
- 2 Samuel 14:14

To all those people who help nurture the human soul

Also by this author:

Reclaiming Eden: Taming the Serpent Ego

INTRODUCTION

As the end of the twentieth century drew to a close, there was great hope in the air that the next millennium would offer us an era of peace and harmony. We thought a new age of enlightenment and peaceful coexistence might finally be here – but the darkest part of mankind's psyche was not ready to die.

The twentieth century was humanity's bloodiest. It began with the Great War, a war to end all wars. That was followed by a flu epidemic which took millions of lives. Then the collapse of the economic system led to the Great Depression, followed by another world war, the Korean War, the Vietnam War and numerous other battles worldwide.

We concluded that century with the Y2K scare – the possibility that all technological systems would self-destruct as the clock rolled to Jan. 1, 2000. Many thought that city lights would fail, planes would crash, nuclear plants would explode, and massive civil unrest would follow.

But it didn't happen. Perhaps, we thought, things would now be different. Maybe everything would start working right, and we could perhaps finally begin to live together as one people on our small planet. We could find the solution to wars, famine, disease, poverty, inequality, and a whole host of problems that have plagued mankind since the dawn of consciousness.

But then on Sept. 11, 2001, it started all over again. Four passenger airliners were hijacked by religious extremists. Two were flown into the twin towers in New York City, one flown into the Pentagon in Washington, D.C., and a fourth crashed into a field in Pennsylvania. The collective dysfunctional ego of radical groups once again spilled out unto the world stage setting in motion a complicated sequence of events that dragged humanity's dark side into our new millennium. Peace and harmony again eluded us.

But this is just the darker side of the story. The other side has to do with the apparent rise in spirituality across the globe. New hope and energy is appearing to counteract the bad. It's not occurring so much in organized, traditional religious institutions, but rather within individuals and among smaller groups. Known as intentional communities, solitaries, or new monasticism, these individuals and groups collectively serve to counterbalance the darker stuff that continues to persist in the world.

Human beings, as many writers have observed, are spiritual beings who happen to be living in a physical world. These two sides, the physical and the spiritual, both strive to gain a foothold in the world. The two realms, intricately interwoven together, are at times in peaceful harmony, and at other times embroiled in great conflict.

The vulnerabilities and immediate demands of our physical state often override the guidance and care offered by the spiritual side. As physical beings, we are driven by survival instincts and basic needs related to safety, procreation, self-esteem, and identity within our social structure. While these physical-world needs are part of life, they are often used by a dysfunctional ego in abnormal ways. Having sufficient security and safety is good, our heart tells us, but having even more is better says our ego! So, we sometimes discover avarice, arrogance, prejudice, or a sense of superiority separating us from others, giving us a false sense of safety and security. We develop illusions that begin to envelop our soul, allowing the problems and issues and attractions of this world to take over our consciousness. Primitive archetypes emerge to command our lives. We begin to lose sight of the moral compass that guides the soul.

The problems of the world are the collective problems of individuals who make up that world. Carl Jung, one of the most prominent psychologists of all time, wrote in his preface to the first edition of *On the Psychology of the Unconscious* in 1916, "The psychology of the individual is reflected in the psychology of the nation. What the nation does is done also by each individual, and so long as the individual continues to do it, the nation will do likewise. Only a change in the attitude of the individual can initiate a change in the psychology of the nation. The great problems of humanity were never yet solved by general laws, but only through regeneration of the attitudes of individuals." He went on to stress that if anything were to change, self-reflection of each person was absolutely necessary. This self-reflection will eventually lead the person to an internal wholeness, reconciling the various parts of his or her psyche. Jung went onto say that the person who learns to deal with his or her own shadow side has indeed done something real for the world, even if only an infinitesimal part.

Long before Jung, Jesus encouraged us to look inwardly to gain an understanding of our inner self. The darker aspects of our psyche are often referred to as "enemies" or "adversaries" in scripture. In Matt. 5:25, Jesus taught people to integrate and harmonize the different aspects of their inner being so that they might enjoy peace. This must start with the individual. Only when the individual becomes harmonized will the world begin to realize its own peace.

The purpose of this book is to bring some of the wisdom of Jesus as recorded in the Gospel of St. Luke into the present day. Jesus was undoubtedly the greatest psychologist of all time, bringing to Earth the loving guidance and wisdom of the

Father. This book is a small tool to help reclaim one's own soul, but an important piece nonetheless. This book does not deal with mental conditions that may be based in genetics, disease, trauma, or poor nutrition. It primarily focuses on the rise of the dysfunctional ego within us, and offers some guidance to taming it. This book is not a substitute for professional counseling, regardless of the issue at hand. We should pursue help from qualified counselors when we need it.

The soul given to each person by God is pure and good. It needs nurturing as it grows in God's love. As we move through life, our soul can get covered up with the mud and grime of living, preventing the soul's natural light to shine through. Spiritual growth is mostly a process of quieting the mind and allowing the heart to receive the goodness that is naturally present and given freely. We are all children of God, and we have all been given very unique skills, talents, and interests to live our lives fully. And while being unique, there is still unity in knowing, loving, and serving God in each and every moment of our lives.

This book contains reflections on each of the sections of the Gospel of Luke. They have been divided as closely as possible to the assigned readings normally found in the Church year when Luke is cited. *It's important to read the Gospel selection first*, and then explore the related reflection that follows in this book. Then, consider discussing it with others who have done the same thing. In some cases assigned readings overlap. Be sure to explore them all.

The common convention "He," "Him" and "His" is used to refer to God, but I do recognize that assigning a gender to God may be presumptuous considering His ineffable nature.

A concluding chapter titled "Bringing it All Together" will help formulate a plan for your life. This chapter contains a set of spiritual principles for readers to consider. These principles are essentially a summary of the material contained within this book. Some material related to care of the soul can be used to develop and maintain your own Rule of Life, should you be moved to develop one.

You'll also find a topical index at the end of the book which can serve to locate related reflections.

If you use these reflections in a small group Bible study, you might want to use one or more of the following questions to generate discussion:

1) Do you agree with this lesson? Why or why not?
2) What is your greatest learning from this lesson?
3) What changes might you make in your life as a result of this lesson?
4) Who can help you with these changes?
5) What else would you like to know about this lesson?
6) How has your understanding of God changed as a result of this lesson?

These questions attempt to evoke responses regarding the balance between a contemplative and an action-oriented life. From a contemplative sense, what does the Gospel passage mean to you? How does it impact your soul? And from an action-orientation perspective, how will it change your life? What are you going to do about it?

Remember that everyone is at a different point in his or her spiritual journey, so take what works for you now and leave the rest. May God be with you on your journey!

Reclaiming Your Soul

LUKE 1:1-25

No Fear in Love

Zechariah, a priest on duty in the temple, was terrified when he saw the angel Gabriel standing near him. Who wouldn't be totally unsettled by such an appearance, especially when it was so unexpected?

Gabriel came to tell Zechariah that his wife, Elizabeth, would have a child who would be named John. But before Gabriel delivered this message, he had to calm Zechariah, so the first words out of his mouth were, "Do not be afraid."

Visits by angels to humans happen a lot in Scripture (as well as throughout history), and just about every time, the angel will first say something like, "Do not be afraid," or "Do not fear."

Fear, even though it is unfortunately viewed as a weakness in many cultures, is an important human reaction to seemingly threatening situations. It's a future-oriented emotion that stems from some potential danger, threat, or uncertain circumstances. We have been given the gift of fear to increase our chances of survival by avoiding or minimizing potential loss of life, health, property, money, family, friends, etc. Fear can quickly evolve into a flight, fight, or freeze response, depending upon the situation.

We are spiritual beings having a human experience. As such, our physical part is vulnerable to nature's laws, as well as the free-will choices we and other people make that can impact our lives. Fear alerts us to danger, and pushes us to respond.

The soul part of us, however, the eternal part, our real self, will survive whatever the physical world can throw at us. It is rooted in the spiritual world where the main economy is love.

The soul was made in love, is nurtured by love, and will be made whole through love.

In the spiritual world there need be no fear. John the Evangelist writes, "There is no fear in love, but perfect love casts out fear; for fear has to do with punishment, and whoever fears does not fully understand love." (1 John 4:18)

What this means to me is that God, who is totally love, is not vindictive or vengeful as He is often portrayed. Rather, He is a God of love who knows each and every person intimately and still loves them despite his or her shortcomings. God's ultimate plan is to bring each person to wholeness and perfection, whether it happens in this world or the next.

Paul affirms this in his letter to the Romans, "For I am convinced that neither death, nor life, nor angels, nor rulers, nor things present, nor things to come, nor powers, nor height, nor depth, nor anything else in all creation, will be able to separate us from the love of God in Christ Jesus our Lord." (Rom. 8:38-39)

LUKE 1:26-38

A Promise Fulfilled

The promise of God to the Virgin Mary in this story is very similar to the promise made by God to King David in 2 Sam. 7, even though the two people lived centuries apart.

In 2 Sam. 7, we hear about the powerful King David who decides to build a temple to honor God, to construct an ornate "house" were God can reside. But God will have none of this, explaining to David through his prophet Nathan (presumably because David wasn't listening) that God does not live in a single house, but lives everywhere. God also declared that it was He who would be building a "house" for David, and not the other way around. The *house* referred to here was the kingdom of the Messiah, a descendent of David. It was to be established forever through God's steadfast love.

Centuries later we read about another similar announcement in Luke 1. The angel Gabriel visits the young maiden Mary, with the message: "You will bear a son, and you will name him Jesus. He will be great…and the Lord God will give to him the throne of his ancestor David…and of his kingdom there will be no end."

Both David and Mary were overcome with joy, and their feelings were recorded in scripture. Mary expressed herself during her visit with Elizabeth in what is now known as the *Magnificat*: "My spirit rejoices…He has filled the hungry with good things…in remembrance of His mercy, according to the promise He made to our ancestors, to Abraham and to his descendents forever." (Luke 1:46b-55)

David expresses feelings very similar to Mary's in the remainder of 2 Sam. 7 (verses 18-29). The covenant with David was also recorded in Ps. 89 where it was written, "…Your steadfast love is established forever…and You built Your throne for all generations…You are my Father, my God, and the Rock of my salvation."

What are the key teachings from these stories?

First, God's love for us is steadfast, and will endure forever. It is unqualified, and unconditional. Paul writes in Rom. 8, "For I am convinced that neither death, nor life, nor angels, nor principalities, nor things present, nor things to come, nor powers, nor height, nor depth, nor any other created thing, shall be able to come between us from the love of God shown to us by Jesus Christ."

Next, the promises of the Christmas story were made ages ago, revealed to us at appropriate times throughout history and through various means, until they were manifested about 2,000 years ago. This is all part of God's plan to bring His children back into His arms someday, fully reconciled, and fully alive.

The complete plan is yet to be fulfilled. Christ came to Earth at the first Christmas (Christmas Advent), and comes to each person in their own heart (Personal Advent). But he will also return one day to complete his plan, and finish making this new heaven and new earth (Return Advent).

God works His plans through both kings and maidens. It doesn't matter what one's role, position or stature is in this world, if anyone is open to His Word, willing to do His will, He'll further His love in the world through that person. Note carefully Mary's words, "Here am I, servant of the Lord; Let it be with me according to your word."

God is not defined by the buildings we build for Him, as David thought. Yes, buildings, pictures and stained glass windows can certainly help us to understand something about God, but His kingdom is not in buildings, it's in hearts. He abides in us and we abide in Him. (John 14)

The Advent season prepares us for the joy and love of Christmas. We enter the Christmas season knowing that the love of God will prevail and make all things new, for as the angel Gabriel told Mary, "Nothing will be impossible with God."

LUKE 1:39-56

The Magnificat

In this segment, we are told of Mary's visit with her cousin, Elizabeth, who was pregnant with John the Baptist. It's reported that John, even while still in Elizabeth's womb, recognized the presence of Jesus, still in the womb of Mary. The spiritual, loving connection was undeniable, and full of joy.

Elizabeth blessed Mary for having faith that God would do what He promised. Mary responded with the "Magnificat," which is the first word of this canticle in Latin. The Magnificat is widely used in Evening Prayer, and actually comes from a collection of Hebrew scriptures (such as 1 Sam. 1:11 and 2:1-10; Deut. 10:21; Ps. 103:17 and 111:9).

People of that day knew their scriptures well. There weren't a lot of other things to study and share, and they had no iPads to connect to Netflix or Facebook. Scripture was studied deeply and reverently, and people knew many passages by heart. Also, the Hebrew Scriptures were full of messianic prophesies and the loving nature of God's kingdom. People were waiting for the arrival of the Messiah, and the things happening to Elizabeth and Mary were clear indications that the time had come. What better way for Mary to express her joy and wonder at this sacred present moment?

While the Magnificat certainly reflected Mary's feelings, the words had a deeper and prophetic reference to Jesus, and what he would bring.

- God's mercy extends from generation to generation.

- He has shown strength through His arm (Christ).
- He won't tolerate arrogance, self-pride or anything that encumbers the soul.
- Those using their power without consideration for other people will be chastised.
- Those who are humble will be raised up.
- The hungry will be filled with good things (not only physical food, but spiritual food as well).
- Those using their wealth foolishly are sent away empty.
- God fulfills His promises.

The coming of Jesus was part of God's ancient plan of salvation for the earth and its *entire* people. God sent His Son to Earth in human form so that we could gain a better understanding of who God is, how much He loved us, and how we could live our lives to the fullest by knowing our own soul.

Christmas reminds us that Jesus Christ is accessible to all of us on a personal one-to-one basis. When we receive him into our hearts and relinquish our false selves to him, we allow our true selves to grow and flourish – we become who God created us to be – unique individuals with special gifts, talents and interests that help us to know, love and serve Him as fully as we can. Then we, too, can declare, "My soul magnifies the Lord, and my spirit rejoices in God my Savior."

LUKE 1:57-80

The Benedictus

For about nine months Zechariah was unable to speak. He was a temple priest and father of John the Baptist, but because he doubted what the angel Gabriel had told him about John, he was silenced until John was born. Now, in the concluding verses of Luke 1, we read that John has been born, and Zechariah's power of speech has once again returned.

Filled with the Holy Spirit, Zechariah then offered a prayer and prophecy, now known as the *Benedictus* (named after the first words of the prayer). The Benedictus, a collection of Hebrew Scripture phrases from what we call the Old Testament, has been recited regularly in Christian prayers throughout the centuries, and will hopefully continue to be used until the end of time.

Why should these few verses receive such esteemed attention? What's in them that's so important?

The Benedictus speaks to the very core of the relationship between God and His people. It reveals the true nature of God's saving grace (as opposed to the many things we've sometimes been told about Him) and what "being free" actually means for us.

The general theme of the prayer revolves around a God of love and mercy (not of retribution and punishment) who looks favorably on His people, and wants the best for them. Through His tender mercy, He wants to place people in a position where they can be truly fulfilled as people, serving God *not with fear*, but with love. To do this, the people need to be rescued from "the hands of the enemies."

On first glance, we think of enemies as other people who hate us, people who carry weapons, form armies, and have a strong desire to invade our land and run things in their own way, sucking up any valuable resources that we may have.

The enemies that the Benedictus refers to are the enemies that we all face *inside* ourselves – the ones that keep us from being fully human. They are things that grow from a dysfunctional ego, such as prejudice, greed, power, hatred, low self-esteem, and arrogance. The seeds of these enemies take root and begin to grow in the hearts of each individual person.

These individual enemies can gather into groups of similar fears and hatreds found in other people. Ultimately these manifest themselves as wars, famines, diseases, corruption, poverty, strife, addictions, waste, pollution, and various forms of violence.

The wisdom we need to battle the internal enemies is given to us by God through Christ. "He has raised up a mighty savior for us..." (v. 69) "...that we would be saved from our enemies..." (v. 71) And then, "...being rescued from the hands of our enemies, we might serve Him without fear..." (v. 74) He will come to "give knowledge of a salvation to his people...(v. 77) to give light (wisdom) to those who sit in darkness (not having the understanding about healthy spirituality and wholeness) and in the shadow of death (fearing things about life and the unknowns of being human)...to guide our feet into the way of peace (inner peace that leads to world peace and harmony)." (v. 79)

God's wisdom can teach us how to deal with our fears, our despair, our grief, and transform these things into gratitude, joy, and faith. Today we can receive this wisdom through Holy Scripture, but also through other people that understand what being human means, such as pastors, therapists, friends, parents, physicians, counselors, spiritual directors. We should not walk our journey alone.

We must come to realize that God our Creator loves us very much, and will do everything possible to bring each and every one of His children to wholeness, one way or another, in this life or the next. You have *nothing* to fear from Him. As Paul wrote to the Romans, "For I am convinced that neither death, nor life, nor angels, nor rulers, nor things present, nor things to come, nor powers, nor height, nor depth, nor anything else in all creation, will be able to separate us from the love of God in Christ Jesus our Lord." (Rom. 8)

This is what the Benedictus is about, and this is why it's used so much as a prayer of thanksgiving and assurance of God's love.

LUKE 2:1-7

Away in a Manger
(Matt. 1:18-25)

What images come into your mind when you think of an all-powerful Messiah, coming to Earth in all His glory with bands of angels, to conquer nations and set the world on a right path? Perhaps you see mountains trembling, or hear thunderous noises, or feel the stomping hooves of warrior horses!

An epic entrance into the world scene such as described above is what it might take to get some people's attention. But Luke 2 suggests quite a different entrance by Christ into our lives. For many people, it's like what happened to the shepherds that first Holy Night: An angel of the Lord appeared to them, and said, "Do not be afraid; I am bringing you good news of great joy for *all* people: To you is born this day in the city of David a Savior, who is the Messiah, the Lord. This will be a sign for you: you will find a child wrapped in bands of cloth and lying in a manger." (Luke 2:12)

You will find a child wrapped in bands of cloth and lying in a manger? This is how a great Messiah makes an entrance into the world? You've got to be kidding!

But as we reflect on the ministry of Jesus, we see how he said and did things that turned people's thinking upside down. It was believed at the time that the Messiah would come with a great army to drive out oppressors – but *this* Messiah came to conquer people's hearts. He sought and fought for reconciliation justice, equality of all genders and races, dignity for everyone – including people on the fringes of society – and an equitable economic system that provided equal opportunity for everyone.

Jesus wanted people to transform their thinking in a new way to be able to accept his challenging teachings. He didn't push for minds that could think at a higher level; he didn't push for more stringent learning standards that required greater mental agility. Quite the contrary, he was asking us to think more simply, more creatively, in a more trusting way that was far more aware of other people and their needs.

He was revealing to us that the path to the kingdom of God was through the mind of a child. "Unless you become like a child you can by no means enter the kingdom of God. Therefore, whoever humbles himself as this little child is the greatest in the kingdom of heaven." (Matt. 18:3-4)

How appropriate that his entrance into our world was that of a child! His first lesson to us was delivered in a manger, before he could even speak. "And this will be a sign for you..." spoke the angel to the shepherds. Every child we see today should serve as a reminder to us of this very important message.

But there's also another message from the manger. How we treat the children in our society is also a direct reflection of how seriously we take the Christmas message. Children represent the foundational work of God: "Whoever receives one little child like this in my name receives me." (Matt. 18:5) We have been taught that if we do good works to the least of these children, then we are doing the works to God.

How well are we doing as a nation? How many children do we leave homeless? How many are abused by their own families? Besides teaching math and science, are we also teaching our children to be sensitive to the needs and well-being of others? When they grow up, will they view society as deeply interconnected, or as an opportunity for individual gain? What do our rewards to the children reinforce? What are we showing them in movies, video games and television? Are we teaching them what love is, and demonstrating it for them in our own lives?

The child in the manger reminds us to become childlike in good ways – being open, curious, accepting, inquisitive, creative, loving and joyful. The child in the manger also reminds us that we need to do something about our society, especially children. We need to take the goodness inherent in our own hearts and move it out into the world, serving God in our own unique way, in the situation that life has for us. To do this we need to reclaim our soul.

LUKE 2:8-20

O Holy Night!

The event that changed history is captured in Luke 2: "And she gave birth to her firstborn son and wrapped him in swaddling cloth, and laid him in a manger, because there was no room for them in the inn." God become united with mankind, binding the two together forever, through the incarnation of God in Jesus.

Why would God do this? Why would He take human form to be with us? Why would the Creator of the entire universe become a vulnerable child in the arms of Mary? The answer to this question is clear: "Because He so loved the world that He gave His only begotten Son, so that everyone who listens to him and believes what he says may find a path to eternal life." (John 3:16)

And Paul writes in Rom. 8, "For I am convinced that neither death, nor life, nor angels, nor rulers, nor things present, nor things to come, nor powers, nor height, nor depth, nor anything else in all creation, will be able to separate us from the love of God in Christ Jesus our Lord."

Christmas is an act of love! Even the angels who appeared to the shepherds that night were filled with immense joy. One angel told them, "Be not afraid; for I bring you good news of great joy which will come to *all* the people; for to you is born this day in the city of David a Savior, who is Christ the Lord." (v. 10-11) A multitude of heavenly hosts appeared with this angel, all praising God and saying, "Glory to God on the highest, and on Earth peace among all people!"

Titus confirms this in his letter, "But when the goodness and loving kindness of God our Savior appeared, he saved us, not because of any works of righteousness that we had done, but according to His mercy, through the water of rebirth and renewal by the Holy Spirit." (Titus 3:4-5) Here we see the Trinity in action: God sends His Son to bring *us* rebirth and renewal through the Holy Spirit. God plus Son plus Holy Spirit equals rebirth and renewal. This is the arithmetic that should be taught in school!

This little baby would soon grow up and begin a ministry of teaching, healing and setting an example of love that would rock the world. Through his life and death, Jesus would prove that God's love for us is real and true, and never-ending. Jesus would teach us that we are all one family of God, and that we are all connected very closely together. If one of us is hurt, we are all hurt to some degree; if one of us is honored, we are all honored to some degree.

We must care for each other, and help each other, and walk with each other along life's path. And although connected together as one family, we are all unique parts in the body of Christ. We need to discover and reclaim our true selves, the soul within each of us that is loving and unique and contains images of God. We learn to shed our false self that encapsulates us, which allows the true self to shine forth in love.

We become reborn and renewed when our true self learns to be who it was made to be in all its uniqueness and diversity. This is the eternal life that we have been given, and is what will continue when we leave this physical world. To know, love, and serve the Lord in our own unique way is the key to joy and fulfillment.

The psalmist writes, "The Lord is king! Let the earth rejoice; let the many coastlands be glad! ... For You, O God, are most high over all the earth..." (Psalm 96) This is indeed the Good News on this most Holy Night.

LUKE 2:15-21

Hallowed Be Thy Name

At some point in our ancient history, people began to refer to each other using specific sounds or words, which eventually became what we call "names." This helped people distinguish each other and provide us with some identity.

If we examine scriptural history, we find ourselves in the Garden of Eden, and learn that the first man's name was "Adam." This is derived from the same root word for earth, or ground – "adamah." It also can mean to be ruddy in appearance, or showing blood in the face (meaning to be alive). Adam got his name from the stuff from which he was made.

Eve came along shortly thereafter, and her name, given to her by Adam, meant that she was the mother of all living beings, a life-giver. So, one of the first things we know about names is that they were generally based on something in nature that was characteristic of the person so named.

Jesus's name was told to Mary by the angel Gabriel. It comes from the Hebrew "Yeshua" and means something similar to "God is help." How appropriate is this name for him! He is here to help us – not to punish or threaten or intimidate. His main characteristic is to help us, to heal us, to show us a way of life that brings us to great inner fulfillment.

There is specialness about names, too. Names gradually become synonymous with the whole person. When someone mentions a person's name, we almost instantly visualize a compilation of what we know about him or her, not just the single characteristic associated with the person's name. This also instantly raises feelings about that person, whether good or bad, and lines up our mental filters which will process any new information coming in about him or her.

Considering where Jesus came from, and what his mission was, his name acquired a sense of holiness and authority. His name also took on an essence of his message of love and compassion, so that when his name is mentioned, we get a calming and reassuring feeling. The name of Jesus carries with it a story about Jesus.

The psalmist sings out, "O Lord, our Sovereign, how majestic is Your Name in all the earth!" (Ps. 8) And Paul writes to the Philippians, "Therefore God also highly exalted him and gave him the Name that is above every name, so that at the Name of Jesus every knee should bend, in heaven and on earth..." (Phil. 2)

His Name is above every name, and therefore the Church sets aside every January 1 to honor it (The Holy Name of Jesus), and to respect it. More than just a name, it carries with it his presence, his power, and his story. "Wherever two or more are gathered in my Name, I am there also." (Matt.18:20) And, "Whoever receives one of these little children in my Name, receives me..." (Matt. 18:5)

Our own name is important to who we are, too. Our name carries with it our life's story, and to know someone's name is to know that story. We don't really know someone until we know his or her story. Our fear of other people diminishes with the more we know. Are we willing to listen? Are we willing to tell our story to someone else?

LUKE 2:22-40

All in the Family

The image of the Christ child in the manger offers us yet another reminder of how God's love for us is revealed. Paul writes in his letter to the Galatians that God sent His Son to us as a redeeming Light, "That we might receive adoption as children." We are no longer slaves to the bondage of the old law, but are now children of God, heirs of His kingdom. Paul adds, "And because you are children, God has sent the Spirit of His Son into our hearts." We can then cry out, "Abba! Father!"

If we are indeed God's children and we can all cry out "Father!" to Him, doesn't that make us all a part of one family?

Simeon was in the temple when the newly born Jesus was brought in to be presented according to Jewish law. Simeon took the baby Jesus in his arms and proclaimed what is now commonly referred to as the *Nunc Dimittis*. "Master, now your servant (Simeon) can depart this world in peace, according to your word; for my eyes have seen Your salvation, which you have prepared in the presence of *all* peoples, a Light to enlighten the Gentiles, and for glory to Your people Israel." (V. 29-32)

The Nunc Dimittis declares a promise fulfilled, it points to the baby Jesus as the source of salvation, and it was meant for *all* people, everywhere. The coming of this baby was the beginning of enlightenment for the world.

The coming of the Son of God to this world on the first Christmas was indeed the greatest gift ever given. It was out of God's pure love for us, designed to show us how to live our lives together in peace, joy and human fulfillment, as a family. Perhaps one of the most important messages the Christmas season can bring us is that all people are, in reality, part of the same family. We are all brothers and sisters under one God, and we have been shown the way we can all live together for the benefit of ourselves, each other, and the world itself.

Why, then, is there still so much strife in the world? Why did Simeon add this dire prediction when he spoke to Mary, "This child is destined for the falling and the rising of many in Israel, and to be a sign that will be opposed ... and a sword will pierce your own soul, too."

When Jesus grew up and began preaching, his message would offend the prejudices embraced by those in power. It still does today. He challenged commonly held ideals, and brought those people on the fringes of society back into his fold. He still does this today, too. He wanted social equity for all people, and stressed equanimity in economics. He antagonized the power interests of the leadership who were prepared to go to any lengths to defend their status and position.

Essentially, Jesus works to turn the world of collective dysfunctional egos upside down. Jesus opposes any system, policy, or ideal that ignores consequences to human lives. This is risky position to take, especially in today's world.

Being a Christian in today's world can expose us to challenges and difficulties. But we can't be fully human unless we become who we were made to be, and follow Christ in our own unique way. The joys of self-fulfillment, however, far outweigh the dangers.

LUKE 2:41-52

The Temple is You

Jesus's parents were returning home from the festival of the Passover in Jerusalem when they realized that Jesus was not with them. Jesus had stayed behind in Jerusalem, but Mary and Joseph thought he was returning home with some of the other travelers. Anxious about his safety, they returned to Jerusalem to look for him.

After a three-day search, they found him in the temple, sitting and listening to the teachers there. When confronted about his whereabouts, Jesus asked them, "Did you not know that I must be in my Father's house?"

This story made me think of all the times I would get frustrated with what seemed to be the absence of God in my life and with the affairs of the world, and wonder, "Where are you, God?" It seemed that if God was where He was supposed to be, there wouldn't be so much trouble in the world. So, I would look and look, and eventually realize that there He was, right there in the temple, right there where He was supposed to be all the time.

But the temple I'm speaking of isn't a building in Jerusalem. The temple in the story is a symbol of the temple Paul writes about in his letter to the Corinthians: "Do you not know that you are God's temple and that God's spirit dwells in you?" (1 Cor. 3 and 6)

Jesus taught us the same thing in John 14 when he said, "You know the Spirit because he abides with you, and will be in you." And in John 15, "Abide in me as I abide in you."

Each of us is a temple of God's Spirit and therefore His love. He abides within us, nurturing our very soul, anxiously waiting for us to recognize Him there, and learning how to surrender to His will for us.

The Savior we were looking for on the outside is waiting for us on the inside. We must learn to look inward to get to know Him, to reclaim our soul, and find out who we are for Him, and then serve Him in our own unique way. This is the answer to our fullness in life; and collectively this is the answer to the world's ills.

LUKE 3:1-20

Joy to the World!
(Matt. 3:1-12. Mark 1:1-8. John 1:19-28)

Six months before the angel Gabriel appeared to Mary, the angel first appeared to Zachariah, an elderly priest married to Elizabeth. Gabriel told Zachariah that he and Elizabeth would have a son, and his name would be John, and this would begin God's plan to visit the earth – in person through Jesus.

Many people would rejoice at John's birth, as he would be filled with the Holy Spirit, and would "turn the hearts of the fathers to the children," and he would turn many of the children of Israel to the Lord their God. (Luke 1:16-17) Note that this implied a direction and commitment of the heart, and was not intended to lay the foundations of an earthly army, something that was hoped for by many Jews waiting for the Messiah.

Zachariah expressed some doubt that the birth of John could even happen, since both he and Elizabeth were "well advanced in years." But as we know, with God all things are possible, and in due course Elizabeth did give birth to John. This prompted Zachariah to express himself in the Benedictus, often recited as part of Morning Prayer services.

The Benedictus fits very well into the Advent season because it speaks of a Savior who is to come, who would save us from our enemies. God would raise up this Savior from the house of David, providing us with the mercy He promised long ago, remembering this holy covenant. Once restored from the hands of our enemies, we might serve Him without fear.

But who are these "enemies" referred to in the Benedictus? And how does this mesh with Gabriel's proclamation that John would lead the way on the mission to change people's hearts?

Certainly in times of war and foreign occupations (in Jesus's day as well as today – will it never end?) people desire to get rid of their oppressors and often call upon God to help them in their cause. Indeed, God may be the only way to bring and keep peace among nations.

Fortunately, all people do not have to face military enemies all of the time, and some people never do. But there is another set of enemies that we all must face at one time or another, and those are the mental and emotional enemies that encumber our souls and keep us apart from God. These, too, are the enemies referred to in the Benedictus.

Who are these enemies? They are the things that encase our soul, things that have been laid on us by social norms, personal experiences, things taught to us that weren't true, and things we've seen others do that we then do, too, but which may not be right. They are thoughts that torment us, that don't belong in our heads because they are not of God. Over the years these thoughts, words and deeds may take the shape of prejudice, bias, shame, worry, greed, fear, inferiority, or attachments to the wrong things; we may even pursue an illusion of power, security, or popularity.

These are all enemies that keep us from a loving relationship with God. But these are also the enemies that God promised to free us from, if we let Him. This is one of the main reasons why God came to Earth – out of His love for us, to teach us, to heal us, to show us how to live together, to save us from the enemies of the soul – "By the tender mercy of our God, the dawn from on high will break upon us (the incarnation), to give us Light to those who sit in darkness and in the shadow of death, to guide our feet into the way of peace." (Luke 1:78-79)

Not just peace between people, but inner peace for each person as well.

Nation would not fight against nation if the people accepted God and had Him in their hearts. We have many people to help us receive God, present day John the Baptists who can "prepare the way of the Lord, making his paths straight." We find them in our teachers, preachers, counselors, physicians, therapists, friends, parents, and siblings to name a few, as long as they, too, have the love of God in their hearts.

LUKE 3:7-18
The Granary of Heaven

"Surely God is my salvation," proclaims Isaiah, "With joy you will draw water from the wells of salvation...Shout aloud and sing for joy!" Isaiah knew that salvation was a good thing. (Isaiah 12:2-3)

So did Zephaniah as he wrote, "Rejoice and exult with all your heart...the Lord has taken away the judgments against you, he has turned away your enemies." (Zeph. 3) He adds further, "He will rejoice over you with gladness, He will renew you in

His love; He will exult over you with loud singing as on a day of festival...at that time I will bring you home, at the time when I gather you."

Even Paul had a good sense of what was to come when he wrote in his letter to the Philippians, "And the peace of God, which surpasses all understanding, will guard your hearts and your minds in Christ Jesus." (Phil. 4:7)

Our own thoughts about salvation sometimes have been shaded by images from great artists' depictions of the Day of Judgment, when the "sheep and goats" will be separated; those being condemned are captured by demon-like creatures and brought to the eternal flames of punishment, while the saints pass through the heavenly gates to an eternal bliss in the presence of God.

Many of the stories we've heard, the books we've read, or the discussions we've had lead us to believe that salvation is an either-or proposition. Either you've run a good race and will be saved by the grace of God for all eternity, or, if you are burdened with unforgiven sins at the point of death, you could spend an eternity burning in the fires of torment.

The exuberant joy expressed by Isaiah, Zephaniah, and Paul over salvation, however, may be because salvation isn't that way at all. They all may have an understanding and appreciation for the human soul, an understanding and appreciation that we've lost somewhere along the way. After all, the soul that God put into each of us was made by Him, and would not be so easily discarded to an eternal landfill.

One clue we have to the meaning of salvation can be found in this segment of the Gospel of Luke. John the Baptist was speaking to the crowds who were wondering if he was the Messiah. John responded that someone greater than he would be coming, and that "his winnowing fork is in his hand, to clear the threshing floor and to gather the wheat into his granary; but the chaff he will burn with unquenchable fire."

On the surface, this appears to be another separation metaphor, like the sheep and goats, with the wheat being the "saved" and the chaff being the condemned. However, it's important to note here that both the wheat and the chaff *come from the same plant.* It's in the winnowing process where the two are separated.

Looked at this way, the salvation process may be more like God taking each of His personally crafted souls and cleaning them up before bringing them into the granary of heaven. Paul says that God will guard our hearts and minds in Christ Jesus. This is the wheat part of us. The chaff part of us includes all the things that have dirtied up our wheat (i.e., our souls), like prejudice, greed, self-pride, hatred, arrogance, worry, fear, shame, false attachments or even feelings of inferiority.

The God of love will do everything in His power to bring *all* His children back home again someday. Cleaning off the soul in the winnowing process may take time for some folks, and may even result in some "weeping and gnashing of teeth." Sometimes people don't want to let go of the things that hurt them. Some people identify with the pain they're carrying, or simply don't see the harm they've done. But the comforting presence of Christ will be there with us, each step of the way, regardless of how long it takes – in this life or the next. We have the comfort of knowing, as Zephaniah said, that "He will rejoice over you with gladness, He will renew you in His love." No soul will be left behind.

LUKE 3:15-22

A Baptism of Fire
(Matt. 3:13-17. Mark 1:9-11)

The story of Jesus's baptism at the River Jordan highlights the difference between John's baptism of water and Jesus's baptism with the Holy Spirit and fire. What's the difference? Why would John only baptize with water, but Jesus would use the Holy Spirit and fire?

The Church's rite of baptism stems from an ancient Hebrew purification rite that used water to cleanse a person who may have become "defiled" by violating some prescribed law. The person in question would be immersed in water, the preferred cleansing agent at the time. There are numerous examples of cleansing in the book of Leviticus.

Baptism continues to have a sense of "cleansing" even today. It's sometimes performed as an entrance rite to the family of God, and signifies a new life in that community.

One way to look at water baptism is that while it has spiritual implications, it's generally meant to begin a transformation of the person with the help and support of other people. A baptism with the Holy Spirit and fire, on the other hand, implies something that goes much deeper, and involves an inner transformation at the hands and heart of Christ.

This idea is further clarified by John's statement in v. 17 of Luke 3, where he adds, "His [Jesus's] winnowing fork is in his hand, to clear his threshing floor and to gather the wheat into his granary; but the chaff he will burn with quenchable fire."

Here we see how this baptism by fire will eventually work. The symbolism of the wheat and chaff tells the story clearly. Each single wheat plant (symbolic for a "person") contains both the wheat berry and the chaff surrounding it. The wheat is the good part, and the chaff is the bad part. Each of us has a little of both inside. The wheat part is to be saved, and the chaff part is to be removed and destroyed.

To separate the two, the winnower (Jesus) tosses the wheat into the air where the wind (the Holy Spirit) separates the two. The wheat, being heavier, falls into a pile, and the chaff, being lighter, falls a short distance away. The wheat is gathered into the barn (the Kingdom of Heaven), and the chaff is piled up and burned until it's gone.

Every person is loved by Jesus. Scripture shows that each person will be brought home to Christ at some point in the future. The chaff of the person will be removed, and the wheat of the person will be saved.

What is this chaff? It's the sum total of the dysfunctional ego that has surrounded the person's true self, the soul. It consists of attachments we may have developed that aren't helpful: attachments to people, things, positions of power, money, and anything else contrary to God's love.

This process, sometimes referred to as the Day of Judgment, will right past wrongs, reveal hidden things, and bring harmony within and between people once again. Pain might be involved as people become aware of the truth of their lives, but the ultimate joy this brings will be well worth the trip. The focus of God will not be so much on people's shortcomings, as it will be on bringing them to wholeness. It is a process of healing, not punishment.

Water baptism begins the process of transformation, but the baptism by the Holy Spirit and fire will bring it to a conclusion, all done out of love by God for all of us.

LUKE 3:23-38

The Ancestors of Jesus
(Matt. 1:1-17)

During Christmas 2013, I discovered that I am not who I thought I was. A 60-year-old belief evaporated when I received an unusual gift from my daughter.

I thought I was half-Swedish and half-German. My grandfather Ivan emigrated from Sweden as a young man with his brother, Victor, about a hundred years ago. Ivan stopped in Wisconsin to marry a Swedish woman, and they eventually settled in the Milwaukee area to raise their family. Victor continued to travel west, and was never heard from again. Ivan and Hilma had nine children, one of whom was my mother.

My great-grandfather Robert Schroeder came to Wisconsin sometime shortly after the Civil War, and married a war widow. He was German, and so was she. One of their sons, Ben, also married a German girl, and my own father was a child of this marriage.

My father and mother met in high school in the Milwaukee area, eventually married, and had four sons, of which I was the third. This, I believed, made me half-Swedish and half-German.

Until I got the present.

Several months before Christmas I was handed a "spit kit" which I could only fill by thinking about a juicy hamburger loaded with cheese, mushrooms, and tomatoes – and a cold brew to wash it down. The vial then traveled to someplace out in California, and I soon forgot about its fate.

Then, near Christmas, I was presented with a report based on the DNA from the vial. The report reflected where my ancestors lived about 500 years ago, before ocean-crossing ships and airplanes mixed things up in a way that even a modern-day Sherlock Holmes would have difficulty sorting things out.

As it turned out, I am slightly less than half-Swedish, and I am also part British, Irish, Finnish, German, French, Middle Eastern and North African. The report also explored earlier genetic routes, and suggested that a few Neanderthals somehow got into the mix (about 3 percent of my DNA code), and perhaps as much as one-third of my genetic material emerged from Doggerland – a now-submerged land mass that once connected England, Norway, and Europe.

Doggerland? Yup. A land rich in mastodons, elk, small game and (probably) mosquitoes. A visit to my homeland is no longer possible, since the glacial warming of 10,000 years ago raised ocean levels and covered it. It has been called the Atlantis of the North.

I knew I had 26 first cousins, but I now was informed that I have more than 900 fifth and sixth cousins around the world. Imagine the summer family picnic we could have!

Interestingly enough, both my spouse and I thought she was 100 percent German. Her DNA test revealed another United Nations amalgam: Scandinavian, French, German, British, Irish, Finnish, Sardinian, and East Asian. Earlier genetic contributors were also Neanderthals and Doggerlanders.

Initially, all this information created a minor identity crisis. Who were we? Should we have lutefisk, wiener schnitzel, or mastodon burgers at Christmas? Should our smorgasbord have a spot for Sardinian eels? Will my wife want yak milk from Mongolia? How will we get along with ourselves considering the state of the world today?

As we thought more about this, however, we began to realize the significance of our genetic diversity. This gift our daughter brought us was more than just a set of numbers and percentages. It reminded us to be careful about the foolishness of elitism, tribalism, and racial superiority. We might be calling ourselves names. Any allegiance to a particular people or nation may be greatly misplaced.

We are all part of an extended family that stretches around the globe. We may have family connections in every country and in every continent. We are truly all brothers and sisters, united as one in the human race. And we are all vulnerable as humans, having the same essential needs of food, clothing, shelter, and community.

Perhaps the lesson from this is that we need to get better connected with each other, share the abundant resources this earth has to offer so that no one is in want, and create opportunities for all our brothers and sisters to become who they were meant to be.

Certainly, Oktoberfest will never be the same.

LUKE 4:1-13

The Temptations
(Matt. 4:1-11. Mark 1:12-13)

After Jesus was baptized in the river Jordan, he was led by the Holy Spirit into the wilderness to make some very important decisions before he began his ministry. His 40-day experience may have been similar to a 40-day Lenten journey we take that is filled with prayer, reflection, discernment, and challenges.

Although Matthew and Luke report the sequence of the three temptations that Jesus faced in slightly different order, they both begin with the devil tempting Jesus to turn a stone into bread to satisfy Jesus's hunger. After all, he had been fasting for 40 days, and was hungry.

Temptations often come clothed in attractive garments. On the surface they seem to make a lot of sense, and may even appear to be a good thing to do. To tempt someone is offensive to God, as it potentially throws a stumbling block in his or her way. To *be* tempted is not a sin. It's quite natural to experience temptations. What we do with them is what counts.

Jesus was being encouraged by the devil to feed himself. So what's wrong with that? On the surface, nothing. Jesus has the power to turn stones into bread, and could have done so. But he recognized the danger of using this power to simply feed the hungry, create better living conditions, or end poverty without addressing the "higher good."

And what is the higher good? Certainly, bread would satisfy basic physical needs, but it wouldn't address the needs of the whole person. Spiritual bread is also needed since we humans are spiritual creatures in a physical body. Therefore his response to the devil was, "One does not live by bread alone, but by every word that comes from the mouth of God." When we help others, we must remember that they are beings of flesh *and* spirit, and should be treated that way.

Then, as Luke reports, "the devil led Jesus up and showed him in an instant all the kingdoms of the world." The devil said that if Jesus would just worship him, all the kingdoms would belong to Jesus.

The people at the time were ready for a military messiah, one who could rally the people together to oust foreign intervention and reestablish a separate and sovereign people. It would have been easier to rise to power on a platform of revolution in response to this need than on a platform of building a world-wide community based on the love of God.

Is there really such a difference between the two systems? God inspired Isaiah to write about this: "For my thoughts are not your thoughts, nor are your ways my ways, says the Lord. For as the heavens are higher than the earth, so are my ways higher than your ways and my thoughts than your thoughts." (Isa. 55:8-9)

Man's natural tendency is to divide. He does so to understand things, to increase safety, and sometimes just out of fear. He forms separate groups for identity and pride. "'If my group is more powerful than your group," he reasons, "then we are safer, and we are better than you." Blind patriotism can be a dangerous thing.

God's natural tendency, however, is to unite. He does so out of love. If we realize that we are all members of the same family, all brothers and sisters, then fear is destroyed, and we can build systems to make sure everyone has enough food, clothing, shelter, medical care, healthy relationships, and other truly human aspects of life. We can help each other become who God made us to be, serving Him in this world in our own unique way based on the special gifts He has given to each one of us.

It's a classic choice we all face today: Should we live according to God's rules, or our own? Jesus knew that ultimately all the kingdoms would be his own anyway. So his response to the devil was "Worship the Lord your God, and serve only him." Perhaps one day we will all become one family, one place where, as Paul writes to the Corinthians, "If one member suffers, all suffer together; if one member is honored, all rejoice together." (1 Cor. 12:26)

Then the devil took Jesus to Jerusalem, placing him high on the temple, saying to him, "If you are the Son of God, throw yourself down from here, for God will command His angels to protect you."

Jesus knew that just because someone wished to follow God's will, there was no guarantee that she or he would be kept from physical harm. Sometimes people assume if they're good enough, they will always have the protection of an angel at their side. But we all know that the world is a dangerous place.

The physical world is set up with a different set of rules than the spiritual world, even though both were made by the same Creator. Natural forces that are part of the creation process are at work. Sometimes we get hurt by these things (earthquakes, tornadoes, lightning, etc.) but when we think about it carefully, most of the world's problems (wars, famines, violence, stress, and some diseases) are actually caused by people making bad decisions. And good people are often adversely impacted by the results.

The certainty in both worlds, however, is that God is ever-loving and steadfast in His mercy, and that eventually all will be made right (two major themes of Julian of Norwich). St. Paul writes that the problems and tribulations we face in this physical world pale in comparison to the joy, benefits, and understanding we will have in the spiritual world.

While this offers some consolation, it doesn't take the full sting from what we sometimes experience. That's where the other benefits of having a relationship with God come in and we have the knowledge that at some point in time, our loving Father will complete His creation and indeed, all will be well.

LUKE 4:14-21

From the Inside Out
(Matt. 4:12-17; 13:53-58. Mark 1:14, 15; 6:1-6)

Soon after Jesus completed his time alone in the wilderness, he began his ministry by teaching in the local synagogues. On one occasion he selected a passage from Isaiah as the basis for his instruction, a passage that summarized the love and compassion that would be the hallmark of his ministry.

The people expected a military Messiah that would expel foreign oppressors from their holy land, and restore the power, peace, and dignity of their people. Their focus was on the physical, external world around them. The way to solve problems in the world, so they thought, was to have the strongest army, the best weapons, and always obey every commandment of God to retain His favor.

But Jesus knew better. Focusing only on externals would never bring a lasting peace or prosperity. It may come and last for a while, but this type of "peace" is not sustainable. Some people would prosper, but always at the expense of others. Jesus knew that to change the world for the better, each person would need to change on the inside first. Once their hearts and minds were transformed, the physical world would change, too.

Jesus read from the scroll of Isaiah: "The Spirit of the Lord is upon me, because He has anointed me to bring good news to the poor." This didn't just mean the economically poor, but anyone who lacked the love and compassion of God.

"He has sent me to proclaim release to the captives...to let the oppressed go free...." People would no longer have to accept the authority of social norms, marketing lies, or the enticement of their own broken egos. They would be free to follow the teaching, wisdom, and love of God. The standard of truth now came from the mouth of God, and not the mouths of men.

"He has sent me to proclaim...recovery of sight to the blind..." Yes, of course, he had the power to cure blindness of the eyes, but here he was talking about being able to see the truth of life. The richness of God's love extends far beyond the physical things we see, the structures that mankind builds, the books that are written, or the pictures that are painted – His love penetrates deep into each person's soul, as well as from the farthest sun to the smallest atom. His love is what fuels the universe in all its parts.

It was part of Jesus's mission to help people "see" the truth – that God is love, that He loves us very much, that He sent His Son to us to teach us how to live in this world, together as one family. Paul writes about this in his first letter to the Corinthians, "For just as the body is one and has many members, and all the members of the body, though many, are one body, so it is with Christ. For in the one Spirit we were all baptized into one body ... and we were all made to drink of one Spirit." (v.12-13)

He goes on to show how all these members of the body (us) are to live together as one body: "The members of the body that *seem* to be weaker are actually indispensable, and those that we think are less honorable we clothe with greater honor, and our less respectable members are treated with greater respect." There should be no dissension within the body. "If one member suffers, all suffer together with it; if one member is honored, all rejoice together with it."

This new ministry would turn the world upside down. The messenger would be loved by some for it, and hated by others.

LUKE 4:21-30

Love Never Ends
(Matt. 13:53-58. Mark 6:1-6)

This reading offers us yet another revelation about God's kingdom. This epiphany disclosed much about the true nature of God, which would greatly please some people, and deeply anger others.

Early in his ministry, Jesus set the stage for what was to come. After reading a passage from Isaiah in a local synagogue, Jesus pointed to two stories where the prophets of God were sent to Gentiles rather than to the Jews (One was the story of Elijah and the widow at Zarephath, and the other was the healing of Naaman the Syrian by Elisha).

Jesus's point was that the love of God could not and would not be contained to just the people who thought they had a special claim on God. God's love was available to anyone who would listen and accept it. No person, or group of people, regardless of their claim, had any special privileges with God. He was open to everyone, equally.

When the people in the synagogue heard this message, they were "filled with rage." They lacked the humility to listen to Jesus, or perhaps they were resentful that this commoner from Nazareth claimed to be getting messages from God. Their false pride built a wall of hatred between themselves and God's love. Right then and there, they wanted to throw Jesus off a cliff.

The reaction against Jesus is quite puzzling, especially when we begin to learn what God's love is all about. Paul offers us some wonderful insights about this in his first letter to the Corinthians: "Love is patient, love is kind; love is not envious or boastful or arrogant or rude. It does not insist on its own way; it is not irritable or resentful; it does not rejoice in wrongdoing, but rejoices in the truth. It bears all things, believes all things, hopes all things, and endures all things. Love never ends." (v. 4-7)

Love creates an even playing field, but some people would prefer to have the chance to stand out, to be noticeably better than others. The illusion of superiority is quite sweet, and catches many flies. This is not to say that doing great things is bad – but if they are done without love, they are hollow acts.

Paul notes in his letter, "If I can speak in the tongues of mortals and of angels, but do not have love, I am a noisy gong or a clanging cymbal. Even if I have prophetic powers and can understand all mysteries and all knowledge, and even if I have faith to move mountains, but do not have love, I am nothing. If I give away all my possessions, and if I hand over my body so that I may boast (spiritual prowess!) but do not have love, I gain nothing." (v. 1-3)

If we can't think, speak, or act with love, then we see in a mirror dimly (only thinking of ourselves), as Paul says. As we become enlightened to the truth, we will begin to see "face-to-face" – we will begin to see the image of Jesus in the other person, and be able to connect to each one, heart to heart. We will also see the image of Jesus in our own soul, and begin to treat ourselves as a child of God as well, for Jesus reminds us to love our neighbor, *as ourselves.*

Present moment awareness, practicing the presence of God, and self-awareness can help us practice love. These tools can help us reflect on each moment of life, seeing where love played a role, and where it may have been missing. It's not always easy to interject love in a world of different values, but it can be done. Having the support of others is very important, too.

LUKE 4:31-37

Demon Attachments
(Mark 1:21-28)

The idea that evil spirits could possess a person may have come from Babylonian and Persian influences, but it was the reality of the people at the time of Jesus. Today, we know that most cases of this type of demon possession are caused by psychological issues, brain trauma, or alcohol and drug abuse.

To some extent, we all face the challenges of staying physically and psychologically healthy. Occasionally, as we walk the path of life, we may find ourselves in need of help to work through some pressing issue in our psyche.

Like minor physical abrasions, there are some psychological bumps and bruises we can usually take care of by ourselves. In more serious cases, we may need the services of qualified professionals to help us get through our issue. It would be ill-advised not to avail ourselves of these services if we have access to them.

Some of the most common forms of "demon possession" in today's world occur when people's egos become so dysfunctional that that they are essentially "totally possessed." This kind of possession usually happens gradually over time as people begin to identify closely with things and ideas of mankind's world – first with one thing, then another, and then another. People can identify with money, power, wealth, titles, status, careers, cars, homes, or even thoughts. "I" and the thing become one.

Each identification (making it "mine") builds an attachment to that thing or idea. That attachment adds another veil over the person's true self (his or her soul), and creates a greater sense of separation of that person from other people.

A fear begins to grow inside – first that the person will not be able to get more of what they want, and then that they will lose what they already have. The need for more and more eventually consumes them and takes over their personality. Their attachments become the focus of their lives.

Interconnections with other people then begin to dissolve. Other people are viewed in one of three ways:
- as a threat; they may prevent further acquisitions, or take away what I have already accumulated
- as a tool; they might be able to help me get more of what I want
- as insignificant; they are neither a threat nor useful – therefore I will waste no time with them

Eventually the true self inside that person can no longer be seen. The public image they project, however, can easily be seen as fake by anyone with "eyes to see." Seeing the true person deep inside is a lot harder – but it's there!

Jesus can see the true self beneath the possessed, false self. He knows the difference, and he knows why that particular demon is in the person. And the demon knows Jesus – the demon knows that it cannot stand in the Light of this truth, and knows that it will be destroyed in his presence.

The man with the demon in Luke 4 cries out "Let us alone!" He uses the plural not because there are many demons, but because the person inside has totally identified with multiple issues and illusions, and they are all now one. "Have you come to destroy us? I know who you are..." it argues.

These types of psychological demons maintain strength by continually creating thoughts in the mind to convince the true self to relinquish its power to the demon. As long as the demon can keep the true self distracted, it can maintain its hold. But if the true self awakens and becomes aware of what's happening, it will regain its hold, and the demon will dissolve.

"Be silent, and come out of him!" commands Jesus. This is the perfect therapy for breaking the bonds of a runaway ego. Transformation begins when the mind is silenced, and the heart is opened to receive. Now the true self, the soul, has a chance to come to consciousness again and realize the foolishness of all those false attachments. It realizes that the only attachments we should have are the ones that nurture the interconnectedness with God and other people. We should attach ourselves to the permanent links that connect heart to heart, and soul to soul, as these are the only ones that have any lasting value.

LUKE 4:38-44

The Runaway Ego
(Matt. 8:14-17. Mark 1:29-34)

In the 1933 movie *Duck Soup,* Groucho Marx plays the role of Fredonia Dictator Rufus T. Firefly, who meets with Mrs. Teasdale to plan a meeting with foreign Ambassador Trentino, hoping to avoid a war between their two nations.

Mrs. Teasdale says, "We both think that a friendly conference will settle everything peacefully. He'll be here any moment."

"Mrs. Teasdale, you did a noble deed," explains Firefly. "I'd be unworthy of the high trust that's been placed in me if I didn't do everything within my power to keep our beloved

Fredonia at peace with the world. I'd be only too happy to meet with Ambassador Trentino and offer him, on behalf of my country, the right hand of good fellowship. And I feel sure that he will accept this gesture in the spirit in which it is offered. [*Here's where the voice in his head, the ego, starts to bellow:*] But suppose he doesn't? A fine thing that'll be. I hold out my hand, and he refuses to accept it! That'll add a lot to prestige, won't it? Me, the head of a country, snubbed by a foreign ambassador! Who does he think he is, that he can come here and make a sap out of me in front of all my people? Think of it! I hold out my hand and that hyena refuses to accept it! Why, the cheap four-flushing swine! He won't get away with it I tell you! He'll never get away with it!"

Ambassador Trentino enters the room, and Firefly complains, "So, you refuse to shake hands with me, eh?" And he slaps the ambassador in the face.

The ambassador turns to Mrs. Teasdale and retorts, "Mrs. Teasdale, this is the last straw! There's no turning back now! This means war!"

Firefly responds, "Then it's war!"

This scenario is certainly a condensed (and somewhat humorous) example of how the ego can overpower thinking, create illusion, and cause problems where there didn't have to be any. Some would say also that Firefly was in a state of possession – possessed by a demon to the point of insanity.

But Firefly's problem wasn't a separate entity that entered his body and took over his mind. His problem was that he failed to recognize that the thoughts being produced by his mind were allowed to run freely, without tethers, and which began to dominate his own decision-making abilities. From the outside, it appears that the person is "not themselves," that something has taken over their minds, that they have a "demon."

In Firefly's case, his mind (which is *supposed* to produce thoughts for you to consider) was sending so much stuff through that he became overwhelmed and began to identify with the thoughts as though they were actually what he believed. He didn't stop to do a reality check of his thinking, but just assumed that because he heard it in his head, it had to be the truth.

The source of this problem is in the voice of the mind – it keeps sending messages that suggests all sorts of possibilities. If we look closely at this idea, there's some survival value in the brain offering us thoughts and ideas. It can serve to keep us aware of not only some unknown potential dangers, but also to suggest possibilities for solving problems or locating needed resources. But unless we recognize and manage these thoughts, they can certainly lead us astray as well. Jesus knew that incessant thinking, the ceaseless inner voice in people's minds, could eventually overpower them, gradually encasing their true self (their soul) in a web of hollow illusions based on fear and false hopes. Identifying with all these thoughts ("these thoughts equal who I am") is how the dysfunctional ego is born and nourished.

So, what was Jesus's main cure for ridding the mind of these mental demons? Silence! If the demon (the runaway brain) could no longer speak, it could not flood the heart and soul with excessive or needless thoughts: "He rebuked them and would not allow them to speak…"

What is our lesson from all this? It's to put reins on the thoughts produced by our brains. And how can we do this? The first and most important thing is to become aware that our thoughts are not coming from our true selves. They are being produced by our brain for us to consider. We are not our thoughts, and our thoughts are not us. The soul is deeply connected to the brain, but the two are not the same.

Once we have created this gap between our true selves and our thoughts, we can accept that we have this brain (which is really trying to help us) and begin to manage the thoughts it produces for us. We can ask ourselves if the thought is really true, and what impact it may have on our true self. We are free to reject any and all thoughts produced by our brain.

We can also reduce the flow of thoughts from our brain in several ways. We can focus on some task, interest or activity, being fully present to what we're doing. This forces the brain to concentrate and leaves it little room for random thoughts. Music is another good method to controlling the influx – listen to an uplifting song and let it run through your head. When that is happening, the brain can't produce other thoughts to disrupt you. Finally, consider a breathing exercise. Focusing on your breathing brings you into the present moment. The brain prefers to reflect on the past, sometimes replaying events in our lives over and over again. At other times, it will wander into the future – planning, speculating, or worrying. The brain is most calm, and thinks most clearly, when it's in the present moment, not the past or the future. Breathing meditations or other focusing activities can help make this happen.

This is all part of the Good News that Jesus proclaimed as he went from city to city. It was Good News for the people 2,000 years ago, and it's Good News for us today. God is love, and He wants to help!

LUKE 5:1-11

Bring Jesus Along
(Matt. 4:18-22. Mark 1:16-20)

I wonder what Jesus taught the crowd that morning along the shore of Lake Gennesaret. His sermon wasn't recorded in any of the Gospels, but he did conclude his talk with a demonstration. He said to Simon Peter, "put out into the deep water and let down your nets for a catch." Even after a fruitless night of fishing, Simon agreed to do it. As a result, they caught many fish.

If this experience with the fish was to prove a point, what might his sermon been about?

Perhaps it was a reminder to keep trying to accomplish whatever it is you're trying to do. The next attempt may be the successful one. But it works better if you bring Jesus along for guidance and direction.

Or perhaps the message was that the greatest rewards for your efforts will be found in the deeper waters – places you have been avoiding because they're too uncertain and scary. But it works best if you bring Jesus along for support and encouragement.

Or perhaps he was telling the crowds that the greater rewards *were* in the deep waters, but just going there wasn't enough. Simon had to let down his nets into the deep waters, or nothing would have been gained. Perhaps we know where to go to get help for something we must work on, but unless we go there with the proper intent and openness of the heart, we will not reap the rewards. But it works even better if you bring Jesus along for mercy and compassion.

Despite Simon Peter's fatigue after a night of fruitless fishing, he surrendered to Jesus's request to try once more, and was greatly rewarded for it. Seeing the amazing results, he knew he was in the presence of some awesome power, great wisdom, and loving compassion. This had a deep impact on him, and he trembled in Jesus's presence. But Jesus said to Simon, "Do not be afraid..."

Jesus wants to be a part of your life. And he wants to do this in a most loving and compassionate way. There is nothing to fear with him at your side. Explore your spiritual journey with him, gently going down new roads, or revisiting old ones in a new way, always with the assurance that he has your best interest in mind. He wants to guide you to the fullness of your being, to become the complete child of God that you were meant to be.

LUKE 5:12-26

Healing from the Inside Out
(Matt. 8:1-4; 9:1-8. Mark 1:40-45; 2:1-12)

Modern medicine is learning more about the incredible link between the mind and body. The power of the mind to help the body heal is being demonstrated every day. We've all heard of the remarkable results of placebo medicines in the cure of both physical and mental illnesses. Some illnesses are even called psychosomatic – physical problems caused by mental or emotional disturbances. How we think about ourselves has a huge impact on how we physically feel.

The connection between body and mind has always been recognized to some degree throughout the ages. In the Hebrew culture of Jesus's time people often believed that physical ailments were the direct result of a person's sins – offenses against God's will. They believed that sometimes the impact of a sinful act would even get passed on down through several generations. The only way to eliminate the physical issues, from their perspective, was to resolve the underlying sin. Forgiveness of the sin, it was believed, could only be granted by God, and would normally follow the proper sacrificial offering through the priests.

But Jesus taught that God does not punish people by causing their injuries or illnesses. This would not be the act of a loving Father. As human beings, though, we *are* vulnerable to many dangers – aging, acts of nature, injury as a result of other people's actions, and injuries we intentionally (or unintentionally) cause ourselves. We can get hurt or become sick just by being human. If a person *believed* that God was punishing him or her for an offense against Him, however, that in itself could adversely impact healing. This may have been the case with the paralyzed man.

The whole idea of resolving underlying spiritual issues within a person before the physical problem can be cured is not far off the mark. If there is indeed such a strong connection between mind and body, it's important to address the person holistically, and not just part of the problem. Certainly, not all illnesses or injuries are caused by an underlying spiritual issue. But having a healthy psyche can be vitally important for the healing of any problem.

Jesus was fully aware of this idea. Certainly, it would be easier to just cure the man of his paralysis. That would involve the manipulation of physical matter. But that wouldn't heal the entire person. The physical healing may not stick if the person's soul was also suffering for some reason. So, Jesus began where he should have, and addressed what he knew was the root issue – the man's spiritual relationship with God. This was restored first, providing him with the necessary foundation for his physical healing.

"Your sins are forgiven you," he told the paralyzed man, perhaps not because the man's sins were causing the paralysis, but because the man *thought* that his sins were causing the paralysis. The man may have committed sins, but God is always looking to heal these sins, not to punish them. This man needed to be put at ease through the understanding that God was not trying to hurt him. The man's soul was set right first.

But this move by Jesus upset the scribes and Pharisees because they believed that only God could forgive sins. This was an opportunity for Jesus to demonstrate to the religious authorities and the people that he was, in fact, authorized on Earth to forgive sins. The paralyzed man, according to the scribes and Pharisees, could not be healed unless his sins had been forgiven. Given the fact that he got up and walked away, his sins therefore *must* have been forgiven! And Jesus did it.

If Jesus had the authority to forgive sins, then it must also be true that he spoke the truth about God. He was indeed sent by God to heal us, teach us, and show us how to live together in peace and unity.

Jesus consistently showed us that the body and soul (the physical and the spiritual) were bound together in a unity that made us a human being. To be whole, there must be harmony between the human side of us and the spiritual side of us. The basis of all healing begins with soul work, and then the cure of physical illnesses and injuries will have a better chance.

LUKE 5:27-32

God Unites, But Evil Divides
(Matt. 9:9-13. Mark 2:13-17)

Body scan machines at major airports have the ability to look right past the exterior of a person and into deeper layers to see what's actually there. X-ray machines have the ability to do the same thing, but are somewhat less controversial. When Jesus chose Levi to be among the twelve disciples, Jesus looked past the visible exterior of Levi to see down deep into his soul. He knew that there was goodness in Levi's heart despite the way that Levi was viewed by the people.

When confronted with the opportunity to follow Jesus, Levi dropped everything and began a new life. He was so thrilled that he "gave a great banquet for Jesus." Apparently a diverse group was in attendance, including tax collectors, Pharisees, and scribes. It seems that the Pharisees and scribes were a bit surprised at the guest list, for they complained to the disciples that Jesus was eating and drinking with tax-collectors and sinners. It was just not acceptable. Jesus must have heard this, because he responded to the Pharisees and scribes that his mission was to bring "sinners" to repentance.

What the Pharisees and scribes ironically overlooked was that Jesus included these Pharisees and scribes in the group that needed repentance.

Jesus sat and ate with people of all kinds because he could look past their surface characteristics and see the God-given soul within each one. Yes, they may have made mistakes; yes, they may have been in trouble; yes, they may have come from lower levels of social classes. But the only thing they wanted to claim in common was their interconnection with each other as human beings, and the abiding nature of God in their hearts. It made them all one.

Jesus was modeling the compassion, dignity and respect of all people, which is part of our Baptismal vows. He was showing us that all people are important to God, and that we must learn to live together in a spirit of collaboration and harmony.

But the Pharisees and scribes present at the banquet couldn't see it. They were able to only see people's surfaces – their physical characteristics, behavior, and social class. They couldn't see deeply into people's true nature. The Pharisees had dysfunctional egos that wrapped their hearts with layers of pride and unfair discrimination. Their unhealthy egos needed to be able to compare themselves with other people, so they looked for characteristics to criticize and demean. That's what makes a dysfunctional ego feel greater and stronger. Ego-based people fear not being special – and yet they don't realize that they would *never* lose their specialness in God's eyes.

But here's an important thing to note: Treating another person with dignity and respect doesn't mean that you simply *tolerate* the other person. To tolerate another person means that you still consider them flawed or inferior, but that you agree to allow them within your personal space. Toleration still maintains a division between people, and is simply veiled with false approval. To view another person with dignity and respect is to view them as a unique equal, just as special in the eyes of God as you are.

We need to practice seeing deeper into people. Much of people's surface behavior can be a projection of a dysfunctional ego, suffering from any number of issues. Think about who is really talking – the person's ego or his or her true self? If God loves all people, how can you not?

LUKE 5:33-39

The New Wine
(Matt. 9:14-17. Mark 2:18-22)

Years ago when I was an employee at a large corporation there would occasionally be a management shuffle, and control of the corporation would fall into the hands of new people with new ideas. We naturally resisted this change, because much of what we did and the way we did it was engrained within our minds and work processes. New ideas always seemed threatening. Would there be staff reductions? Would we be able to do the new processes? Would our customers accept the changes? Would our jobs be downgraded to lower pay? Anxiety grew as the change became closer to reality.

We can certainly understand some of the concerns that the religious leaders of Jesus's time had when Jesus appeared on the scene and began to preach and teach his perspective on what religion was supposed to be all about. The things Jesus was telling people appeared to threaten the power and prestige of the religious leaders; Jesus preached equality of economic class, gender, and race. He taught that we are all precious in God's eyes; that we are all interconnected with each other and with God Himself; that Jesus was the vine, and we are the branches receiving nourishment from him.

Jesus's purpose was not to destroy the foundation of the Judaic culture; he merely wanted to take it to the next level. "Think not that I have come to destroy the Law or the Prophets; I am not come to destroy, but to fulfill." (Matt. 5:17) The early Law and Prophets provided some fundamental guidelines for a young nation to establish itself, and it worked. The people were now ready to go deeper into what humanity was all about – to learn more about the spiritual nature that is within all of us.

This was "new wine" being produced for the people. It required a new wineskin – the new commandment that Jesus gave to us, to love one another as he has loved us. This expanded the perspective on what society was supposed to be about, on what living together was supposed to be about, and on what leadership was supposed to be about. The old wine – the old practices – had grown into its own power structure that failed to integrate the physical nature of people with their spiritual nature. Something more was now needed.

Those who had been drinking the old wine (those in power) would resist this new teaching – the change was threatening to them because they would lose their position and control of the people under this new philosophy. These leaders had become fully identified with their roles; their dysfunctional egos had full possession of their mental faculties. "The old is good," they would declare, and they would confront Jesus whenever possible to thwart his movement. Eventually they came to the conclusion that the only way to stop him would be to kill him. So they did. (It would be important to point out here that we, as employees resisting change of new management in the corporation, did not go this far to stop its progress!)

The new wine was certainly a change for the better for some people, and could have been for all, if everyone had "eyes to see and ears to hear." Even today, there is resistance to living a truly Christian life and having a Christian society. The separation of people, one from another, would dissolve, and the understanding of unity and equality of people would be the guiding principle. That doesn't mean, however, that the uniqueness of each person would be overlooked; rather, it would be celebrated!

We have much to learn yet about the new wine, and there will always be some resistance by those who are comfortable with the taste of the old wine. "The old is good," they will declare, "and we do not need the new." The new wine, however, is our path to enlightenment.

LUKE 6:1-5

A Grain of Truth
(Matt. 12:1-8. Mark 2:23-28)

One day Jesus was walking through a cornfield with his disciples and a few others on a Sabbath day. Because some of the disciples were hungry, they plucked a few grains and ate them. Since this was considered to be "harvesting," the Pharisees complained to Jesus that the disciples were violating Sabbath law.

The Law was given to a young Hebrew nation to help it grow and become a thriving society. But over time the Law became the ruler rather than the Guide. The path to God, as thought by some groups, was to obey every law and its authorized interpretation to the letter. The closer people came to obeying every law, the closer they would be to God.

Even today we see systems and rules becoming more important than the people they were designed to serve. It happens in government, in corporations, and in special-interest groups, to name a few. Systems that mankind create take on a life of their own, overshadowing the very purpose for which they were made in the first place. This is what gradually happened to the Pharisees. They tried to follow all the spiritual rules and laws in an effort to show their respect and love for God, but the rules and laws became more important than the reasons they were originally created. What was made to serve the people became something that the people had to serve.

Jesus brought a renewed purpose for the law based on the understanding that people have both spiritual *and* physical needs. Human beings have both a physical part (the *human* side) and a spiritual part (the *being* side). We are a unique blend of two realms.

Jesus knew that for a person to be whole, these two sides must be in harmony. If either side had a pressing need, it could throw the entire person into dissonance. Hunger is a good example. Food is a basic need of all humans. When we are hungry, we think of food. When we are hungry, we are less able to concentrate on other things, like spiritual matters. There is no shame in being hungry – the shame is when mankind's systems and practices prevent that hunger from being satisfied properly.

Jesus considered people's physical needs before he tried to teach them anything. Sometimes he would even feed thousands of people who came to hear him. He healed people's injuries and sicknesses while he taught them. He knew that there was no shame in being human; he knew that even spiritual rules could get in the way of spiritual growth if they didn't address basic human needs.

So when the Pharisees objected to the disciples taking some food, Jesus pointed out that even David and his companions ate bread that was only supposed to be eaten by the priests. Jesus capped it off by strongly suggesting that he, as the Son of Man, made the rules about the Sabbath.

How well does our society address the physical needs of its members? How well does it address the spiritual side or the psychological side?

LUKE 6:6-11

When the Good News is Not Good News
(Matt. 12:9-14. Mark 3:1-6)

The good news of God's Kingdom is not good news for everyone. Surprisingly, some people find Jesus's egalitarian message of love and compassion to be threatening and disruptive. In fact, the good news eventually led some people to have Jesus killed.

Many of the teachings and healings of Jesus perturbed those in power at the time. In Luke 6, Jesus heals a man with a withered hand on the Sabbath. Normally this was not allowed by rabbinical law unless it was an extreme case of need. This healing by Jesus represented a change in the way things were structured. It brought a threat to those in power who had control over the people.

But it wasn't just *this* healing that led them to plot Jesus's death. Jesus had been increasingly undermining their system. He violated Sabbath laws, attacked those in power, and taught that people were all equally important in the eyes of God. Jesus gave people a hope and purpose that they never had before. He gave them a sense of worth, and a direct line to God that was previously reserved only to the elite.

But how do the imbalances of power and resources happen in society in the first place? Why do some people work to acquire more than they actually need?

Even though we humans are part spiritual, we're also living a physical existence, and therefore we have needs for safety, food, social order, identity and physical comforts. All these things are very uncertain in this world; we are vulnerable physical creatures – our health, our property, our friends, our family, and our very lives are vulnerable. This lack of certainty gives rise to a natural sense of fear; that is, we have fear in the present about potential losses in the future.

Fear is a strong emotion and a powerful motivator. There's a natural survival value to fear, but it can become dysfunctional when it creates a significant scarcity in resources for some and reserved opportunity for others. This is one of the things Jesus warned against. Dysfunctional egos create tribalism in many forms, constructing social and economic divisions that benefit some people at the expense of others.

But Jesus taught that we are all children of God, each person unique but equal in God's eyes. Paul reminded us that as a body of Christ, when one person suffers, we all suffer to some degree, and when one person is honored, we are all honored to some degree. (1 Cor. 12) We are to love our neighbor as Christ has loved us.

In a world of abundant resources, we spread a fear of scarcity. But most of the scarcity centers on things that are *wanted*, but not really *needed*, and we often confuse the difference. Somehow, we don't really believe that there is enough for everyone, so we end up with the very lopsided system we have today where just a few people in the world have more than half of all the people.

John writes that "there is no fear in love, but perfect love casts out fear; for fear has to do with punishment, and whoever fears has not reached perfection [full understanding] in love." (1 John 4:18) To love each other without fear is a risk we all must take. It's the right path for the body of Christ.

LUKE 6:12-16

Decisions, Decisions
(Matt. 10:1-4. Mark 3:13-19)

Jesus had an important decision to make – or rather, twelve of them. He knew that his earthly ministry would end at some point, and he needed people that he could trust with his mission and spread his teachings after he was gone. This was a make-or-break decision – if he chose the wrong people, then everything he worked for, everything he gave up (including his life) may have been for nothing.

It was a difficult decision for Jesus, and he wanted to get it right. Which of the disciples would be faithful in carrying out the mission? Who would serve God's purpose best? Who would best represent the compassion and love God had for His children?

When faced with a decision as important as this, Jesus knew that it was critical to think it through carefully, and make a connection with the Father who could guide him. He had to clear his mind so that he could connect with God. He had to be able to listen with the ear of his heart.

To do this, Jesus went up on a mountain to be alone and pray, to a place where there were no distractions, a place where he could have time to discern his choices. Prayer, as he taught us, was listening carefully to what God had to say. God's guidance to us is usually not heard from a cloud or a thunderbolt, but more often as a whisper or a sensation in the heart. It usually happens in a silent space.

At dawn, Jesus had made up his mind with God's help. "He called his disciples together and chose twelve of them, whom he named apostles: Simon, whom he named Peter, and his brother Andrew, and James, and John, and Philip, and Bartholomew, and Matthew, and Thomas, and James son of Alphaeus, and Simon, who was called the Zealot, and Judas son of James, and Judas Iscariot." A disciple was a follower, a student. An apostle, however, would be a trained disciple, one who would go out on a mission.

But even with all this careful planning and prayerful discernment, something still went wrong. Judas Iscariot, one of the twelve, ended up betraying Jesus to the authorities in exchange for thirty pieces of silver.

Why did this happen? How could something go this wrong when the decision was carefully made with God's help?

The volatile free will of mankind creates an underlying uncertainty in life's plans and sometimes leaves us scratching our heads in bewilderment. The best plans crumble before our very eyes.

Why does free will – the freedom to choose our own way – exist?

Because God is love, and He wants us to be loving, too. But love *must* be a choice, or it can't be love. If we're programmed to love, or forced to love, then it isn't love. So, for human beings to be able to love, they also must be able to reject that love with their God-given free will. This is a risk that must be taken if love is to exist.

So, regardless of how well we plan something out, regardless of the careful thought and discernment we put into a decision, there's always the possibility that the human element of free will may disrupt our expectations. With humans involved, the chances that something will go exactly as planned are not good.

Does that mean we should not plan or pray? Certainly not. Things would be far worse if we didn't give some thought and care into the choices we make, or fail to bring God into the discernment process. We can gain some great insight into a decision by using the best methods and tools we have available – it's just that there are some things for which we can't plan at all.

We do the best we can with what we have. And we must remember that things might not go our way. Things might change course at any moment, but the resources for making the best of any situation are usually present in that very moment if we sharpen our awareness, patience, and resolve. God is always ready to help.

LUKE 6:17-26

On Earth, As It Is In Heaven
(Matt. 4:23-25; 5:1-12)

The main concern of original Christianity, as it has been presented through the life and ministry of Jesus, is personal transformation and social reform. It's God's desire that we build a society here on earth that reflects the values and wisdom He offered to us through the teachings of His Son. Again and again, Jesus lobbied for personal health, economic equity, social justice, peace on earth, and personal salvation from oppression of all kinds – psychological, political, economic, legal, religious, military – whatever.

We hear this message yet again in the sixth chapter of Luke, sometimes referred to as the "Sermon on the Plain." Similar to the beatitudes found in the Sermon on the Mount in Matthew (and probably based on the same source document), Luke's version focuses on some key components of Jesus's call for social order, with particular emphasis on wealth and economics.

Jesus mingled with all kinds of people, many of whom were considered "sinners" by religious officials, and therefore to be shunned. But Jesus always looked past the sins of anyone who sought him, and stepped right into their heart and soul. They came to Jesus to be physically healed, so he healed them. They came to him to learn, so he taught them. They came to him with troubled and unclean spirits (usually referring to anguish, fear, despair, grief, and related psychological issues), and were cured. People felt this loving power and yearned for it.

Luke then records Jesus's pointed remarks about economic inequality. "If you are poor," he taught, "things will be made right in the kingdom of God. And if you hunger now, you will be filled in the kingdom of God. And if you weep and mourn now, you will be comforted and will laugh again in the kingdom of God."

Then he issued a warning to those who are at the high end of the economic scale, and probably exploiting the system: "Woe to you who are rich, for you have [already] received your consolation; woe to you who are full now, for you will be hungry; woe to you who are laughing now, for you will mourn and weep."

We must not think that Jesus was against wealth or those who were fortunate enough to have it. His concern was the misuse of wealth, usually brought about by a system that favored one group over another that left some people having less than they needed for essential living. Jesus said that everyone should have basic food, clothing, shelter, community and opportunity. If a person is able and willing to work, but there isn't enough work to do, they are still entitled to a living wage, every day. No one should be without enough to live on.

In a Huffington Post article written on Jan. 20, 2014, Oxfam reported that the top 85 richest people in the world have the same amount of wealth as the poorest 3,500,000,000. (This is about half of the world's population!) This is a blatant example of the inequity that Jesus talked about. It's a gross injustice of the distribution of God's resources.

At least two things must now happen. First, those who have more than they need must begin to divest themselves of their surplus loot, and secondly, the rest of us must work to change the way the system works so that these sinful imbalances are not perpetuated into the future. If these changes are not going to happen willingly, then the rest of us must seek change within the laws to replace the anemic, silent morals of the unresponsive rich.

This is the call we hear from the words of Our Lord's Prayer: "Thy kingdom come, Thy will be done, on earth as it is in heaven. Give us this day our daily bread..."

God's passion is to use the systems of heaven here on Earth in the society of mankind. There is much work to do.

LUKE 6:27-36
Love Will Keep Us Together
(Matt. 5:38-48; 7:12a)

Jesus left us with a new commandment: "Love one another as I have loved you. By this shall all people know that you are my disciples, if you have love for one another." (John 13:34-35) This, above all else, is the cornerstone upon which Christianity is built. Everything we think, do, or say, should be contributing in some way to this ideal.

To get anywhere with this proposition, however, we need an operational definition of "love." What does it mean to love our neighbors as ourselves?

There are many different types of love, and there have been many books written about love. But one definition that seems to stand the test of time, and is in keeping with the foundational intent of Jesus's wisdom, is that to love someone is to help him or her come to the fullest realization of who he or she was meant to be. The Merriam Webster Dictionary defines this love as "unselfish loyal and benevolent concern for the good of another."

Love is not only just making sure that your neighbors have all the essentials of living: food, clothing, and shelter, but also helping them discover why God made them, what gifts and talents they may have been given. Love is doing what you can to nurture these things in them. This is, of course, different for every person. Therefore love is not trying to get another person to be just like you, do the things that you do, or like the things that you like. It's allowing and encouraging them to grow into their own spiritual identity to the fullest.

But to be effective at this we also need to love ourselves, and this is why the Great Commandment instructed us "to love God and your neighbor, as yourself." We must be growing in our understanding of love to be able to help others. Personal transformation in a loving way was one of the key points of Jesus's message. Once we know what love is all about we can then begin to reach out to others – even our enemies – in a loving way, and really mean it. Jesus's wisdom first transforms us, and through us begins to transform the world.

Jesus's ministry was totally dedicated to the purpose of teaching us how to live together in this world. He devoted his entire life to this cause, doing whatever he could to show God's passion for us. In this way his life became a kind of sacrifice, being obedient to this purpose, even if it led to his death.

In Luke 6, Jesus offers us some further explanation about this love. True love, he explained, reaches beyond just those who love us. It must go out unconditionally to anyone, regardless of who they are. We don't necessarily have to like the person, especially our enemies, but we must still try to nurture them in a loving way. Who knows? As we all grow in love we may actually learn to like each other, too!

LUKE 6:37-45

The Tree Can Change
(Matt. 7:1-5; 7:17-20; 12:34b-35)

We Christians often make the claim that God is love. But in making this claim, we place ourselves in a somewhat vulnerable position when it is quite clear that much of the world, which is God's creation, is not a very loving place at all. With wars, famines, diseases, pollution, corruption, greed, oppression of many kinds, financial struggles, homelessness, and a multitude of other social ills, we can't help but wonder sometimes if we're just fooling ourselves. Who are we trying to kid?

But let's not forget the basics at play here. To be sure, God *is* love. God loves us unconditionally, and wants us to love, too. This is the path to a wholesome and enriching life, not only for each of us as individuals, but for the world as well. This is one of the main purposes for Christianity – personal transformation at the hands of Christ that leads to world transformation, all based on love.

Love, however, is a choice. If it were programmed into us it wouldn't be love, it would be software, and we would be robots. We must *choose* to love...or not. And this choice can only happen if we are given free will – the power to choose. So, if God wants us to be loving, He must take the risk and give us free will.

A good parent, though, would not stop there. That would be like giving a child a set of car keys and a car without adequate instruction. True, even with proper training the person may still violate traffic laws and create some dangerous situations (just look at drivers today!) but at least the person would have a better foundation upon which to make decisions.

God, too, has provided us with good instruction. Throughout the years we have been given the Law of Moses, the wisdom of Jesus, and the Holy Advocate to teach us in our hearts. We've also known some people in our lives who have been good teachers and counselors. But even with all that, we can still choose ill will instead of God's will.

Jesus knew this, too: "The good person out of the good treasure of the heart produces good, and the evil person out of evil treasure produces evil; for it is out of the abundance of the heart that the mouth speaks." We know that the good tree bears good fruit, and the bad tree bears bad fruit.

But the tree *can* change! Bad trees *can* become good trees and bear good fruit. Jesus said we can "first take the log out of your own eye, and then you will see clearly to take the speck out of your neighbor's eye." So it is possible to change – if we want to.

Personal transformation begins with a change in heart. We turn the corner back to God when we decide to put away our old ways and begin to live the new. We must realize that whatever is wrong with the world is part of our own deepest self. To change the world we must accept this and then begin to change ourselves. So with a fresh intention, we begin to learn new ways, new thoughts, new perspectives that will enable us to "sing a new song with our lives" as the psalmist writes in Ps. 96.

The transformation of our lives can happen both from the inside out and the outside in. In the first way, we study about God, we pray daily, we meditate, we listen to our teachers, we consider, we evaluate, we assess. We learn personal self-awareness and practice the presence of God.

In the second way, from the outside in, we actually practice behaviors that are loving so that we learn what they feel like, and how they impact other people. Jesus gave us plenty of examples – some of them in today's passage: Do not judge, do not condemn, forgive, and find ways to help others.

Build a team of good advisers who can help you on your journey. We weren't meant to travel alone. Practice, practice, practice! And don't be afraid of falling down now and then – it's getting up again that counts.

LUKE 6:46-49
Building a Foundation
(Matt. 7:24-27)

This little parable in Luke 6 is fairly straight forward – if you don't have a strong spiritual foundation based on the love of God, then you'll have a poor chance of surviving life's more challenging times. The house represents the life one builds for oneself, and the foundation is the principles by which one lives. Supporting a strong foundation is the Rock – the Rock of Ages, being Christ. To "dig deeply" is to pursue the knowledge and love of God with great interest and enthusiasm, practicing one's faith moment by moment, and strengthening it against the trials (floods) of life.

The thing that isn't quite as easy to understand is why some people don't act on the Word when they hear it. "Why do you call me 'Lord, Lord', and do not do what I tell you?" asks Christ.

A perplexing thing, indeed. But there are reasons for it, and they all begin with people's freedom to choose their own path in life – and this freedom to choose must exist for a very good reason. God is love, and He wants a loving world filled with loving people. But for love to exist, it must be a choice, or it can't be love, because love cannot be forced. Therefore, human beings must have free will. And of course, some people will choose love, and others will not. That's the risk God takes when bestowing free will on His children.

Still, the choice to follow the wisdom of God must be influenced by certain factors swimming around inside the mind of those making the decision. What are some of these factors? As we know, Jesus himself met with great resistance to his teachings by some of the people in authority. Why? Because his teachings would upset the current status quo. Those in power would have to share it so that everyone had an equal voice. Those with excess wealth would have to share it with those in true need. Social classes and prejudices would crumble; gender, age, economic and racial inequality would dissolve. It would cost some people all the things that fed their dysfunctional egos; things that fed their illusions, their power, and their prestige. It would change the material foundation they were building to protect them against the uncertainties of life. It offered a spiritual foundation that seemed less certain and harder to understand and to trust. It's no wonder that they ultimately decided that they had to stop this revolutionary Jesus however they could.

The same things that influenced people in Jesus's day still influence us today. We have uncertainty and fear about life, so we sometimes seek power, fame, money, and prestige in hopes to survive. We build a protection against life's threatening floods with a foundation of social and material strength. This can also feed our dysfunctional egos, which seek the illusion of superiority. But this isn't Rock – it's sand – and it won't stand the test of time. Mankind's way often creates divisions between people and inequality of social and economic systems that were meant to serve everyone. An imbalance of goods and services for some people always leaves others deficient.

Today we also have other things that distract us from exploring the riches of God's wisdom. The busier we become, the less chance there is for us to awaken to this loving wisdom. We have activities scheduled from early morning to late at night. We're pummeled almost every waking moment with messages from multiple devices: personal computers, televisions, radios, iPhones, roadside billboards, newspapers, junk mail, telemarketing calls and even bumper stickers. It can be overwhelming. We are not equipped to take in this much information from so many different sources. The world changes so fast we don't have time to try to fit our personal value systems into the new order of things. It's easy to get swept along by this raging flood.

Our challenge in today's world is to create enough space in our day, moment by moment, to fairly consider the value of a spiritual foundation. Where will we place our "treasure"? Where will we place our hope? Where will we send our hearts? To properly discern these ideas, we need space. We need quiet times. We need some solitude. Then we must choose the best course for our lives. We must cast aside the expectations of an overachieving society and begin to reconnect with our spiritual roots where the materials for a solid foundation can be found.

Life does indeed have its floods. We've all experienced them. God wants us to have the best foundation we can build to weather these storms, and it can only be found in God's love and wisdom.

LUKE 7:1-10

Humble Authority
(Matt. 8:5-13. John 4:43-54)

A Roman centurion had a servant who was ill. He valued this servant highly, and when he had heard about Jesus, he sent some messengers to Jesus asking him to come and heal this servant.

The centurion was a man of great authority, commanding other soldiers to do whatever he wished. He could have easily sent his soldiers to force Jesus to come and heal his servant, but he yielded to Jesus's authority instead. "I am not worthy to have you come under my roof; therefore I did not presume to come to you." Recognizing the power of Jesus, the centurion merely asked, "But only speak the word, and let my servant be healed."

Often when people reach positions of power and authority it "goes to their head." This means that their ego begins to identify with this position, leading to an overinflated sense of self-worth. Earthly power can be very alluring. When a person of position has a weak spiritual foundation, she or he is easily seduced by the illusion of superiority.

This centurion displayed a remarkable sense of true self, however, and recognized the proper place for earthly power and prestige. Jesus was very pleased at the centurion's level of awareness. Even though the centurion possessed earthly power and authority, he was able to keep things in perspective. Apparently the centurion knew there was another realm, a spiritual realm that was far greater than what could be found on Earth.

Finding a person of humble authority in today's world is a rare treat. How can a leader lead others and still keep a proper level of respect and humility? How can that person keep from getting buried in illusory power and position?

It begins with becoming aware, becoming conscious of the difference between the mind (which is the home of the potentially dysfunctional ego) and the soul where the true self can be found. When people learn to separate their thoughts from their identity, and know that they have a stronger foundation in God than what mankind has to offer, then they begin to expand their consciousness and sharpen their sensitivity. This sensitivity then allows them to see past other people's egos straight into their true selves. They are more tolerant and understanding, and have much greater ability to assess situations at hand.

The centurion's awareness allowed for the power of Jesus to do its work. There was no resistance, and no blockage to Jesus's healing power. When the messengers returned to the centurion, they found the servant in good health.

LUKE 7:11-17

New Life from Old

One of the themes we find in literature throughout recorded history, and in many cultures, is the idea of rebirth, or new life coming from old. Sometimes this archetype, if you will, emerges in a story of someone being brought back to life who has, in some way, physically died.

Two stories in scripture involve a widow with an only son who has died. The first is described in I Kings 17, where Elijah resuscitates the son of the widow of Zarephath after praying to God. The second case, recorded in Luke 7, involved the widow of Nain, who was escorting the body of her son out of the town. Jesus had compassion on her, and restored her son's life. While these stories are hundreds of years apart, they point to a basic truth about life – new life can, indeed, spring from old.

Both of these stories remind us of a third case, where a widow watched her son, Jesus, being executed. The only begotten Son of God was eventually restored to life by the love of God despite the hatred of his accusers.

The existence of life after physical death is well-established. It's the way things have been designed. Life is so precious that, even though it may change form, it continues under the protection and love of God.

These stories demonstrate the life-giving power of God. But we must also realize that it doesn't just stop at physical existence. People can die spiritually, too, by succumbing to the ever-growing ego. Like Saul of Tarsus, a person can get buried under the burdens of prejudice, hatred, fear, shame, worry, and numerous other illusions. These things can become "scales over our eyes," blinding us to truth, joy, unity and peace.

The psalmist knows that spiritual resuscitation comes at the hand of God: "The Lord sets the prisoners free; the Lord opens the eyes of the blind." (Ps. 146)

Paul writes about his spiritual awakening in his letter to the Galatians. He describes his earlier life as spiritual death: "I was violently persecuting the Church of God and was trying to destroy it." But Paul was called through the grace of God, the scales fell from his eyes, and he was reborn. The one who formerly persecuted the Church was "now proclaiming the faith he once tried to destroy." (Gal. 1)

Jesus teaches us that God is present when "the dead are raised up." (Luke 7:22) This idea can refer to physical healings and resurrections, it can refer to the transitions people experience passing from this life to the next, and it can refer to people awakening from the dead spiritually.

It's in God's sweet nature to heal, preserve and enhance the life that He gives. We will experience this in many ways as we travel through time that never ends. We will come to know His good intentions, steadfast love, and how He makes new life from old.

LUKE 7:18-35

The Justice of God
(Matt. 11:1-19)

When we think of 'justice' in today's world, we often think of it as the bad person getting caught and being punished for his or her crime. We make the criminal pay for the crime, sometimes with monetary fines, sometimes with a period of incarceration, and sometimes both. Our sense of justice carries with it a sense of 'getting even.' It's a *punitive* type of justice, and its roots go far back into our ancestry.

But there's another kind of justice that is often overlooked, especially in Western society: The justice that Jesus taught, which encompasses a lot more than we're used to. It's called *restorative* justice.

With restorative justice, the offender is still apprehended and charged with the offense, and may even be found guilty. And yes, there still may be restitution, but that's just the beginning. The idea behind restorative justice is to actually make things better for *everyone* – to bring about a greater wholeness and unity in society than there was before the offense.

Restorative justice, like punitive justice, seeks the apprehension and prosecution of the offender. In addition, however, restorative justice contains a number of other factors.

- It includes restoration of the injured parties to a condition similar to what they had prior to the offense (sometimes sought in punitive justice cases, but all too often falls short of full restoration).
- It offers some sort of replacement services or support provided to those offended, if the damage or injury is permanent; support would be provided first by the offending party, if appropriate, and then by the community if the offending party couldn't or shouldn't provide it. (This is the meaning behind "an eye for an eye" – if I blinded someone, I must arrange to serve as their eyes; it doesn't mean that I would be blinded, too.)
- It assesses the possible causes and reasons *why* the offender committed the offense. This assessment is sometimes referred to as a $360°$ review – all possible factors that might have contributed to the offenders actions are examined: family life, school, friends, neighborhood environment, peer pressure, nutrition, whatever it may be. Of course, this doesn't shift the responsibility for the offense. After all, the offender committed the offense and must answer for it. But some of that responsibility is shared with society. (See the last bullet point below.)

- It sentences the offender in a way that considers the above factors. Punishments are not fixed by statute, but are determined by a trained jury or panel of advisors. The sentence *might* include incarceration, especially in cases where offenders are a continuing danger to themselves or others. But it could also include therapy, relocation, a change in environment, a change in diet, more education, or whatever is needed to position this person from ever *wanting* to commit an offense again.
- It ensures the contributing elements to the offense also come under scrutiny. To some extent the social structures within which the offender grew up might have contributed in some way to the offense. If there's a way to make these better and stronger, then it should be part of the resolution of this case. Are there ways to improve the mental health systems, to improve the schools, or to improve our understanding of nutrition or other factors?

The idea is that we not only learn from our mistakes, but we put a higher value on the person and his or her relationship with other people. We become fully aware of the interconnectedness of people with each other and the earth. We come to understand that every person is a human being, and that means that no one is totally good or totally bad. Luke writes that the justice of God means, "The blind receive their sight, the lame walk, the lepers are cleansed, the deaf hear, the dead are raised, the poor have good news brought to them."

Carrying this concept forward to the Great Day of Judgment, we begin to see that God's justice will be the foundation. Many of us have been taught that this will be a punitive type of judgment and justice; that people will either be "saved" or they will be condemned to hell forever. But what Jesus taught and demonstrated was that God's justice is restorative. God's justice is based on compassion, mercy, and love.

It's God's plan to bring everyone home to Him and restore them to wholeness and unity. It's a time of healing and reconciliation – not punishment and torture. The Day of Judgment will be a time of evaluation and determining how the person can be restored to what he or she was truly meant to be. For some people, this may take a long, long time – but there *is* an eternity to get it done!

LUKE 7:36-8:3

Deep Love

We live in a fast-paced society that often leaves our time and space filled with many things and activities, all of which we only experience briefly and at a very shallow level, like a flat stone skipping over the surface of the water. Scurrying from one thing to the next, the depth of our lives and our understanding of life itself is replaced by an illusion of fulfillment or accomplishment. We never grasp the implications of our thoughts, words, and deeds on the underlying fabric of life, relying instead on valuing the worth of things and moments in time in terms of their surface value.

Nathan tried to enlighten King David whose understanding of the true depths of life were being diluted by his power and delusions. David had Uriah killed so that David could take Bethsheba for himself, a foul act for which he had little awareness of its implications. (2 Sam. 11-12)

Nathan told David that there was once a rich man who stole a lamb from a poor man, and prepared it for a guest who had traveled to visit the rich man. The rich man did not want to take a lamb from his own herd, so he took it from the poor man. In terms of the law, the rich man forcibly transferred the value of the lamb from the poor man to himself. If it went to court, the rich man should be expected to at least reimburse the poor man for the value of the lamb. Perhaps there would also be a monetary fine and a lecture, but then things would be settled. The rest of us, in our busy lives, might agree that the test of "eye for an eye" was met.

In reality, however, much more damage had been done. Consider the real worth of the lamb to the poor man. There existed an intense bond between this lamb and the family: "It grew up with the man and his children; it used to eat of his meager fare, and drink from his cup, and lie in his bosom, and it was like a daughter to him." No amount of money can replace this type of loss.

The lamb's owner experienced and understood the love that flows between God and His children and creatures. The awareness of this connection and the great value of a life together were rooted in the depth of his soul, which could only be reached through reflection, present moment awareness, and a willingness to understand. This lamb was extremely precious to the poor man – but was just meat to the rich man. The rich man was shallow, and was blind to the true nature of things.

Upon hearing the story, King David's eyes were opened and he began to understand the depth of the situation. He began to actually feel the pain of the poor man, and declared that the rich man deserved to die. When Nathan explained that David's offense was like that of the rich man, David finally experienced the true consequences of his actions. He felt the pain that he inflicted on someone else.

In Luke 7 we see yet another example of someone who lived only at a shallow surface level of understanding. The Pharisee Simon had invited Jesus to dine with him, thinking that Jesus was a great prophet. It would enhance Simon's prestige to have dined with a man like Jesus.

A woman, a known sinner, showed up to minister to Jesus. Simon the Pharisee became disappointed that Jesus didn't recognize her for what she was and permitted her to remain and minister to him. The law was clear to Simon – this woman should not be here, nor should people of respect have anything to do with her – apparently Jesus was no prophet after all.

But Jesus actually saw this woman much more clearly than did Simon. Jesus saw this woman for who she really was – someone who understood the depth of life and the full implications of her actions, like King David. Now she was looking for forgiveness at a very deep level, from the only person who could deeply forgive. She knew that Jesus's love could go anywhere that evil was present, anywhere there was hurt and pain, and meet it head on to heal it.

Jesus asked Simon, "Do you *really* see this woman?"

People who can see deeply into life have a unique gift of sensitivity, like Nathan and Jesus; they can see and understand the true implications of a misplaced thought, word, or deed. They know how much hurt and pain occurs that cannot be compensated for in a court of law. And because of this knowledge, they are more careful about what they think, do or say. They do not want to inflict this deeper pain on anyone or anything – because they love.

LUKE 8:4-15

The Sower and His Seed
(Matt. 13:1-9, 18-23. Mark 4:1-9; 13-20)

I had two strawberry patches in my garden one summer, just a few feet apart from each other. The strawberry plants in each patch were the same variety, and all were in their second year of service. The plants in one of the patches, however, were large, and were producing big, red, sweet berries. The plants in the other patch barely grew, and the berries, when they appeared, were the size of peas.

Gardeners and farmers know that there are many factors in place before plants will grow and produce their offerings. The weather must be fine, there must be enough moisture in the soil, the soil itself must have the right balance of nutrients and organisms to support the plants, and there must be no predators (insect, animal, or otherwise) to harm the plants as they grow. The gardener's and farmer's job is to try to arrange for all these factors to be in balance. Gardeners and farmers can't make the seeds germinate or make the plants grow – that's part of Nature's realm – they can only set the stage and nurture the plants for optimum results.

The Word of God is high-quality seed. When planted, it can grow and provide the most beautiful fruit, and its roots can dig deep, providing a strong foundation against life's rough times. But even the seeds of God must have fertile soil to grow, and must be protected against the adverse influences that can thwart its success. Jesus warned us of these challenges in his parable of the sower.

The sower (God through Christ and the Holy Spirit) went out to sow his seed. This seed represents the wisdom and love of God as given to us through the Word. It's offered to us to help us live a full and enriching life, in collaboration with other people. When lived collectively, it can literally bring heaven to Earth, as we often request from God in the Lord's Prayer, "Thy kingdom come, Thy will be done, on earth as it is in heaven." This can only be done through the acceptance and application of God's Word in our lives.

So, why don't we have heaven on Earth now? After all, Jesus came to us more than 2,000 years ago, and we should have gotten it together by now, right?

Well, the same things that endanger the plants in my garden also endanger the seeds planted by God. Sometimes the Word of God gets planted right in front of us, but we're too busy with earthly things to notice, and so it gets trampled. Other things are more attractive and enticing, and therefore garner our attention more quickly and hold us fast. The birds of the air (other demands on our time and resources) are quick to snap up the seeds and consume them. The Words just may not make sense for us at this time. We have been given the free will to choose, and we do!

Other seeds of God fall on rock, and wither for lack of moisture as they try to grow. The 'rock' in this case is indifference, apathy, or lack of awareness. These are things within our own minds that don't allow the roots to take hold, or don't allow any nurturing of the ideas and wisdom from the Word. This resistance may stem from a dysfunctional ego that has grown over one's soul, fed by fear or uncertainty about life.

And some seeds from God fall in places where there are also thorns growing – other influences that smother the goodness offered by the seeds. Local influences are too strong for the person to resist, so they follow the path of the thorns.

Fortunately, as Jesus pointed out, some of God's seeds do fall on good soil, and do grow well, and produce "a hundredfold." This is what keeps us going; this is what keeps the Word alive and the hope for heaven on earth. Many of the early Christians expected it to happen rather quickly, but over time realized that the process would be on God's time. We know that to be true today, too.

We must also remember that there's not just a one-time chance for people to capture the Word of God. People change as they go through life, and at some point may be more ready to receive the Word than they are now. The Great Sower never stops sowing, never stops trying. The seeds are abundant and persistent.

A brief comment is in order concerning Jesus's statement, "To you it has been given to know the secrets of the kingdom of God; but to others I speak in parables, so that 'looking they may not perceive, and listening they may not understand.'" Most commentators agree that it was *not* Jesus's intent to make the Wisdom of God unclear to some people and clear to others. It seems from one perspective he was actually saying that he used parables to make the message more understandable to some people who were "hard of heart." There may have been a bit of frustration or even sarcasm in his words, like "Even if I painted some people a picture they still wouldn't get it!" It might also be that Luke took some liberties in crafting this insertion into the text.

Whatever the cause or reason behind this statement, remember that Jesus wanted everyone to receive, accept, and live the teachings he brought from God. Also, every person certainly is at a different place in life, and not everyone is ready to accept Jesus's message.

LUKE 8:16-21

The Light of Love
(Matt. 12:46-50. Mark 3:31-35, 4:21-25)

When God decided to make the earth, the first thing He created was Light. This action ensured that the world would be filled with the Light of love, that love would be the guiding force, and that this love would never end.

Light has an interesting property. If we hold a glass prism up to a beam of sunlight, we discover that this natural light is actually a blend of all colors – in essence, a united rainbow. The Light of God is not just one color, but a perfect blend of many colors, all at different frequencies. Take any color and follow it back to its source and you'll find God.

Light has other properties, too. It shines on anyone, whether or not they are considered to be "good" or "bad" people. Any person can step out into it and enjoy what it has to offer. This light charges nothing for its services, and demands nothing in return. It simply exists to shine on anyone willing to receive it.

This light loves to shine! It wants to give freely of itself because it is the key to all life on Earth – without it the plants would die, and the world would grow cold and dark.

John teaches us a few things about what he calls the Light. He explains that Jesus was like light, too – "In him was life; and the life was the light of people." (John 1:4) Jesus himself said, "I am the light of the world; he that follows me shall not walk in darkness, but shall have the light of life." (John 8:12)

It is clear that when Scripture speaks of light in this sense, it speaks of the love and wisdom with which God enlightens us. God is the lamp that lightens our path. We can't see miles down the road of life, but only the next step or two, and that is enough as long as God is with us.

In this passage from Luke 8, Jesus tells us that this light can't be hidden. It must be present for all to see; a beacon, an invitation for others to welcome it into their lives. This light creates new connections, a new family, for Jesus points out that his real brothers and sisters "are those who hear the word of God and do it."

This light is for you; this light is for everyone.

LUKE 8:22-25

$1 + 1 > 2$
(Matt. 8:23-27. Mark 4:35-41)

When I was still young (*many* years ago) our family spent some vacation time at my grandfather Ivan's cottage in northern Wisconsin. There were many lakes nearby, and it was always tempting to take out a boat and try some fishing. Weather forecasting in the 1960s wasn't as good as it is today, so it was always something of a gamble to go out too far.

On one occasion my brother Charles and I were out in a small motorized boat when a storm quickly developed – similar to the boating situation described above in Luke 8. Gentle waves turned into whitecaps and the partly sunny sky became its own sea of gray and black clouds, twisting and rolling in a menacing fury as they raced over the tops of the swaying trees along the shore.

Charles promptly started the small motor and headed back toward shore. "Get to the front of the boat and watch for hidden stumps!" he yelled. I leaned out over the front of the boat as we went faster and faster, straining my eyes into the murky, churning water. I couldn't see a thing. "What would happen if we hit a stump?" I wondered. I didn't want to know. I carried an unfair responsibility and I was frightened. Lord, help us!

Danger is something we've all probably faced at one time or another. It creates a genuine fear for survival, for self-preservation. This type of fear is a gift. But fear occurs in a variety of forms, such as anxiety, worry, nervousness or general discomfort. Sometimes it digs very deep into our hearts. Without adequate support and understanding, fears can grow well beyond their intended purpose.

In the face of their danger, the disciples called upon Jesus who was with them in the boat, even though he seemed unconcerned in his sleep. "Master, Master, we are perishing!" they yelled as their fear boiled over into despair. The Master awoke, rebuking the wind and raging waves, bringing calm once again into their lives. Then he admonished the disciples for not having enough faith.

Not enough faith? What did that mean? Were the disciples supposed to believe they had the same abilities as Jesus? Were they supposed to be able to rebuke the wind and the raging waves, making them calm like Jesus did? Anyone who thought that Jesus meant that the disciples did not have enough faith to control nature might have been left feeling a little bad about themselves. "I don't have enough faith to control nature like Jesus, so there must be something wrong with me!"

But this isn't what Jesus meant when he admonished the disciples. He was sleeping in the boat as they struggled with the storm because he knew that they should be able to handle it without him. Jesus had more confidence in them than they had in themselves. He knew that together, as a team, they would be able to get through the threat together. That's what he was trying to teach them. But their fears got the better of them. Jesus admonished them for *not having enough faith in themselves as a group*. In life, one plus one always equals more than two. Together, with other like-minded people, we can draw strength, we can pool resources, and we can encourage each other and share hope.

Keep in mind that for a group effort to be effective, however, certain conditions must be present. Note, for example, the phrase above: "like-minded people." The disciples in the boat, although having different personalities and different backgrounds, all had the same vision. They had the same long-term mission – to learn and spread the Word of God – and they had the same present-moment goal – to get their boat safely to the opposite shore. They weren't pulling in opposite directions, and they shared a common threat.

They also had something else with them – the Presence of God in Jesus. To travel without him at their side would seriously jeopardize their mission. He gave the disciples values and wisdom with which to live and work together. He provided them with the leadership they needed but didn't always recognize. He displayed complete confidence in their abilities by actually sleeping in the boat while they battled the storm!

We face many challenges together in life that we can resolve if we come together as one, keeping the wisdom and guidance of God close at hand. Rather than having to calm the storm, we can become calm within the storm. Let us recognize how the power we have together is multiplied in knowing, loving, and serving God.

LUKE 8:26-39

Today's Demons
(Matt. 8:28-34. Mark 5:1-20)

When God gave mankind free will to love, He more than likely also extended this option to spiritual beings which we commonly think of as angels. It could be that some of these spiritual beings chose not to love, and subsequently fell from grace. Hence, the appearance of what people throughout history thought of as 'demons.'

In Jesus's time, a person who suffered from some form of mental illness was sometimes thought to "have a demon." It was a way to explain unusual and aberrant behaviors that were little understood as they are today. But we humans face other types of demons – the ones that emerge from the shadows of our minds, sometimes growing to such a degree that it almost seems like they possess us.

In Luke 8, Jesus and his disciples encounter a deeply troubled man who was reported to be possessed by many demons. He refers to himself as "Legion," because he is troubled by so many things. As a result, he runs around naked, lives in a cemetery, and is subject to loud outbursts that can be quite disturbing to others.

A person in today's world faces more demands on his or her interests, resources, and time than ever before. We are pulled in a multitude of directions by numerous influences that can significantly impact who we are. And these influences are more present than ever before, too, thanks to the technology that brings it to us – personal computers, 'smart' phones, radio, television, and the many avenues of social media. We live in fertile ground for developing and nurturing mental illnesses.

It's no wonder that we can become unglued, especially if we don't have a strong spiritual foundation to hold it all together. As these messages and pressures overcrowd our mental processing systems, it's possible to get confused and distracted. We might feel so torn by all the conflicting interests and demands that they begin to fracture our identity and we reach a point that we "don't know what to think anymore." Some of our issues seem to get so large that they take on their own identities, such as persistent pain memories that grow into hatred or prejudice or needless suffering. A dysfunctional ego may emerge and envelop our true selves, blocking much of the goodness and love that would normally be there. We become possessed by this ego and may not even know it. It wants to live and grow and survive in its own form, seeking things that give it identity and attacking those things that threaten it. It rants and raves against the very forces that could help it. The present-day demon has arrived.

The demon-possessed man knew that Jesus had the power to heal him. But sometimes healing comes at a price – the healing process often starts with some pain; the pain of cleansing, the pain of bone setting, the pain of stitching a wound, the pain of realizing the error made or a wrong committed. "What have you to do with me, Jesus, Son of the Most High God? I beg you, do not torment me" cried the man with demons.

It's only through the love and compassion and the power of God that we can restore our mental health. This happens when we, like the demon-possessed man, sit at the feet of Jesus to hear his wisdom and council. In today's world, this love comes to us through those people trying to help us on our journey, as well as our own time spent in prayer, meditation, and contemplation. They're all used to fill our minds and hearts with the Presence of the loving God.

Attention to mental health has diminished so much during the last several decades that we are now facing a mental health crisis. We must not neglect this very foundational piece of being human or we will continue to struggle with violent crime, wars, depression, addictions, anxiety, loneliness and fear along with a multitude of other symptoms. The core of our being is our soul, and we must give it the attention it deserves.

Then, perhaps, one day we, too, can return to our home and declare how much God has done for us like the man in Luke 8.

LUKE 8:40-56

Holy Interruptions
(Matt. 9:18-26. Mark 5:21-43)

Many of us have experienced times when we have been given an important assignment or made part of an exciting project – perhaps at work, through church, or for some large family event. It seemed that all our energies were now focused on this task, and much of our time and energy was spent on achieving the final goal. Our own reputation was challenged as well, so we wanted to get things right.

So off we go, busily working, when the inevitable interruption occurs along the way. Someone stops to say hello, or just kill time. Maybe the phone rings in the middle of a great thought. We might feel irritation or frustration because we've been distracted, and the project (and our public image) is now in jeopardy. We become torn between the need to work on the project or mission, and the demands of the present moment.

On one occasion Jesus was approached by Jairus, an important leader of the synagogue, who begged Jesus to come and tend to his dying daughter. Jesus, with his usual compassion for anyone in trouble, accepted the mission and started off toward Jairus's house. A serious mission indeed! A high-level Jewish official had a family member facing death – the urgency and implications to Jesus's ministry were evident.

As Jesus proceeded toward Jairus's house, and with the crowds pressing in all around him, he felt someone come up behind him and touch the fringe of his cloak. "Who touched me?" he asked, which perplexed the disciples because there were people all around pressing against him. Jesus was probably touched by many people, they thought.

The sensitivity of Jesus, even in the face of an urgent task, helped him to recognize that at least one of the people who touched him also had an urgent need. But who was it? Having been discovered, a woman revealed herself to Jesus, admitting her action because of her need. She was a humble woman, desiring to stay hidden among the crowd. But compelled by her long-term illness, and hearing about the healing powers of this man Jesus, she felt that even touching the hem of his cloak would be enough to cure her.

Jesus delayed his mission to Jairus's house because of this present-moment interruption. He stopped and spent some time with the woman, and assured her that because of her faith, she would be well. Her twelve years of trouble came to an end. Jesus then resumed his mission to help Jairus's daughter.

A mission of high order contained within it a holy interruption. We may not always realize it, but often God gives us things to do for totally different reasons than we think. Often the end result of a project or goal is not as important as the human interaction that happens along the way. Sometimes the real purpose of the project or task is merely to put us into contact with someone else who is in need, *or* who may be able to help *us* with a problem. We may have accepted a mission of a high order that leads to a holy interruption – the true reason for our journey in the first place.

Interruptions in daily life may actually be holy encounters, planned by God to bring us together in surprising and unique ways to help each other, person to person. Yes, completing a project or task is important, but too often we overlook the treasures along the way. We miss them because our eyes are focused too far into the future, and we blind ourselves to the present moment. Without the sensitivity of awareness to the present moment we often miss the jewels at our feet.

Being "sensitive" to other people's needs is not often valued in our Western society. To be sensitive is often considered a sign of weakness, a hindrance to getting things accomplished, and yet it was one of the most powerful attributes demonstrated time and time again by Jesus. Amid a busy crowd of people pressing in on him as he walked, he instantly felt the slightest brush of a person in need. Oh, what a wonderful world this would be if we could all do this!

Holy interruptions are not to be dismissed, but are to be explored. What are the needs of this present moment? What can I do to make this moment better? What is God offering me right now?

LUKE 9:1-6

Humility
(Matt. 10:5-15. Mark 6:7-13)

One of the key themes in Luke 9 is humility. The text seems to suggest that humility is needed *to be able to do* God's work, and it's needed for us to *receive* God's blessings.

Paul writes in 2 Corinthians that if he became too "elated" over the exceptional character of the revelations he received, people might reject him, and perhaps would even turn away from his message. Or, Paul himself may inflate his message beyond what it should be. "Therefore," he writes, "to keep me from being too elated, a thorn was given me in the flesh, a messenger of Satan to torment me, to keep me from being too elated."

We don't know what this "thorn" was, whether it was something physical or psychological, but it reminded Paul of his place in the overall scheme of things – he was part of the overall plan and play of God, nothing more, nothing less. Paul felt that his power was made perfect in his weakness.

Jesus also warned his disciples not to get too distracted with excessive "creature comforts" in life when they went out on mission work. He ordered them to take nothing for their journey "except a staff; no bread, no bag, no money in their belts; but to wear sandals and not to put on two tunics." He was sending them a message never to let their desire for comfort take their attention from their mission. He knew that the ego could get in their way.

When Jesus went back to his hometown, people took offense at him because they thought he was speaking way out of his place. "Where did this man get all this information?"

they asked. "Who is this guy? What are his credentials? When did he graduate from Harvard Divinity School?" As a result of the *people's* hubris, Jesus was not able to do much good there. He was blocked.

He also warned his disciples when he sent them out on mission that if the people refused to hear the Gospel message (after making a persistent effort to reach them), the disciples were to "shake off the dust that is on your feet as a testimony against them," and then go somewhere else that the message may be heard.

So, what is humility? Merriam Webster's Dictionary defines it as "the quality or state of being humble."

OK, so what is "being humble?"

Webster's goes on to say that to be humble means to not be proud or haughty. It means not to be arrogant or aggressive. Being humble is to reflect, express, or offer ourselves in a spirit of deference or submission. It means ranking low in hierarchy or scale.

Frankly, this definition is only partially satisfying. It seems to miss the full intent of humility.

The origin of the word humility stems from the word *humus*, or earth. Interestingly, the word 'humility' comes from the earth, and so do we: "And God shaped man from the soil of the ground, and blew the breath of life into his nostrils..." (Genesis 2:7)

Maybe 'humility' means to be more connected to and understanding of our place in the grand scheme – that we're not above or below other people, or nature itself – but a part of it. We didn't make ourselves, but were made by a loving God.

Maybe we lose our humility when we lose our sense of place; when we think we're better than someone else, or more powerful than nature. Maybe we lose our humility when we think that we are *less* than we really are! (I like to refer to this as our "e-stop" as opposed to our "e-go.")

Humility is what is left over after the false self has been shed. The more we come into God's Presence and God's Grace, the more our false self, our dysfunctional ego-self, dissolves. Humility is a natural characteristic of the true self, the soul, which God placed in each of us.

We grow our humility through daily prayer, reflective study, and personal service to others.

LUKE 9:7-9

Power Corrupts
(Matt. 14:1-12. Mark 6:14-29)

Herod heard all that had been done by Jesus and his disciples – the healings, the preaching, and the teaching. What they were doing all seemed to be a good thing, and yet Herod failed to recognize it as such. He had already executed John the Baptist, following his arrest for opposing Herod. And now Herod desired to stop Jesus, too.

But why? Why would anyone want to interfere with Jesus's message of love and unity among people? Simply, the power and authority of Herod was threatened. Jesus taught social and economic equity. He taught that all people, all races, are children of God and deserved the same respect, honor and dignity. No one was better as a person than anyone else, and no one was worse as a person than anyone else. Each person had unique gifts that, when used with others, could accomplish amazing things.

Herod would not encounter Jesus until shortly after Jesus's arrest. Jesus was brought to Herod, but Herod only used his soldiers to mock and abuse Jesus. Then he sent Jesus back to Pilate to determine Jesus's fate.

People in power must use their power to serve others. Power is not to be used for one's own good, but for the good of everyone. But people in power usually develop strong self-serving egos that will vehemently defend their position and authority. Sometimes even to the point of murdering those threatening them.

Jesus knew that his message would bring divisions among people, even though its intent was to unify people: to bring them together under a common banner of love, compassion and equity. He warned the disciples when he sent them out that he was sending them like sheep into a world of wolves. What they taught would sometimes set father against son, and mother against daughter. Whoever thought that they would lose something under Jesus's way of life would naturally oppose his message.

Herod eventually got his way – Pilate allowed Jesus to be crucified so that he was no longer a threat. But we know that the outcome was much different. Through Jesus's death and resurrection, we have the assurance that, as Paul declared, nothing can come between God and His love for us – not even death. (Rom. 8:38-39) Jesus then became the Christ, and his power extended to the ends of the earth.

LUKE 9:10-17

Feeding the World
(Matt. 14:13-21. Mark 6:30-44. John 6:1-14)

The story of the feeding of the 5,000 was captured in all four Gospels. It was a significant event, and there has been much discussion by commentators down through the ages about what it means. Was this a demonstration of Jesus's power over nature? Was it a thawing of the hearts of the multitude so that they shared food with others? Or was it reflecting some of the early symbolism of the Holy Eucharist celebration?

If we step back a bit and look at the event holistically, it's quite probably a blend of all three lines of thought, leaving us with a powerful message for living in today's world. The truth rarely fits into one box.

John the evangelist claimed that Jesus was the channel through which God created everything: "All things were made by him; and without him was not anything made that was made." (John 1:3) If so, then Jesus Christ does have the power to turn stones into bread. So, the feeding of the thousands could be demonstrating this fact.

And yet in today's world, great nutritional inequity exists. Some people have too much food and other people are dying of starvation. Is Christ sleeping? Doesn't he care? Why doesn't he use these powers to straighten things out like he did in the story?

Yes, he cares, and yes, he is fully awake. The problem is that *we're* not fully awake. We're not conscious enough to fully realize our place in God's kingdom, our place on this earth, and our place with each other as a family of God. Too often as humans we think we're separate from everything, that we're above nature and not part of it. We see life as a game of survival where we rush through it, trying to accumulate more stuff than the other guy. And we seem to idolize those people who acquire lots of stuff.

Something must bring us together, to awaken us to the fact of our interconnectedness with each other and with the world, and that we are all equally important in the eyes of God. But if we try to unite the people of the world through religion we will fail. Religions created by mankind express culturally biased interpretations of scripture and experience, and therefore we'll always be in disagreement about what is or isn't "right."

So, how can the story of the feeding of the thousands help us? What does it have to teach us?

The story is trying to teach us that the key to bringing unity and equity to the world is working together for the good of *all* people through love. That's the only thing that will work. The story teaches us an important spiritual lesson. "Man does not live by bread alone, but by every word that comes from the mouth of God," declared Jesus to the devil. (Matt. 4:4)

The story reminds us that Jesus *has* the power to multiply loaves and fishes to feed his people; but it also teaches us that Jesus wants *us* to do it together as a family instead, using the resources that he has provided on this earth. There is enough to share, and there will be some left over – but we must do it collaboratively in a loving manner.

We can see elements of the Holy Eucharist in the story, too: "And taking the five loaves and the two fish, he looked up to heaven, and blessed and broke them, and gave them to the disciples to set before the crowd." Miraculously, it seemed as though the five loaves and two fish multiplied enough to feed the thousands!

But let's also remember that when we celebrate the Holy Eucharist today, the bread and wine are brought to the altar by the people at the start of the service. The gifts of God, offered by the people of God, are given back to the people of God. Carrying some bread and dried fish around would not be unheard of back in Jesus's day. There weren't many fast food restaurants or street vendors when people went out for a day's journey into the city, so they would sometimes take a sack of food. When the people saw the holy sharing that began with the five loaves and two fishes, they were moved to join in with what they already had with them knowing that more food was needed. The softening of their hearts was the true miracle!

This is what Jesus hoped would happen. He wanted us to learn that collectively, as a family of God, we could accomplish things together. By doing so, we might realize that we were meant to live collaboratively, caring for each other. He created an abundant world, but we must learn that it's meant to be shared. This is one of the foundational lessons we are reminded of during Holy Communion.

LUKE 9:18-36

The Law and the Prophets
(Matt. 16:13-28, 17:1-8. Mark 8:27-9:8)

Two powerful themes wind their way through Luke 9, coming together into a unified plan for each one of us.

The first of these themes is the affirmation of Christ as the One Unifier between the law and the prophets. The Hebrew Scriptures gave us two great theological aspirations: finding God through obedience to His rules and regulations, and building a personal relationship with God through realizing His presence in our souls.

Moses is considered to be the great law-receiver, coming down from Mt. Sinai with the Ten Commandments. From this event sprang many rules and guidelines found in Leviticus and Deuteronomy, developed by the priestly class. Many people believed that the path to salvation was to be found in perfect obedience to these laws. This was quite evident in the lives of the Pharisees in Jesus's time.

But some prophets of the Old Testament saw things a bit differently. They tried to promote a path to God through developing a personal relationship with Him. The prophets knew that God was all-present and all-knowing, and took a very personal interest in people's lives. Even the psalmists began to understand God as being something better than a militant autocrat.

Now we come to the transfiguration on the mountaintop, when Jesus took Peter, John, and James to this place to pray. During this episode, the countenance of Jesus changed, and Moses and Elijah appeared in glory with him. They talked together, and were glorified together. It was a symbolic event that positioned Jesus as uniting the law and the prophets into one idea; that the love of God is for everyone, and the law can be used as a guide to show us what that love means.

Jesus often said that he did not come to destroy the law, but to fulfill it. All law must be interpreted and applied according to God's love, or it is worthless, and could very well become a worshipped god itself. The law is not the end, but a means to the end, which is God's love.

But the love of God does not stay on the mountaintop. Unless it's applied in community, it has little value. Therefore we come to the second great theme of the readings – Jesus and his inner circle came down from the mountain and went back into human society, with all its frailties, shortcomings and problems.

Here, the law and the prophets come together for the common good. Here, we take what God has given us, no matter what it is, and apply it in our own unique way to the present moment situation. We shed the baggage of the past, leaving it to God's loving mercy, and we shun the fears and worries of the future, leaving them to God's providence. Now we are free to blend the guidance of the law and the love of the prophets into our own lives.

The psalmist writes, "Extol the Lord our God, and worship at his holy mountain." (Psalm 99:5) This is the *contemplative* side of our monastic profession. Jesus says, "Love your neighbor as yourself." (Mark 12:31) This is the *action* part of our monastic profession. Do both for balance. Do both for fulfillment. Do both for the love of God.

LUKE 9:37-43a

The Mountain and the Valley
(Matt. 17:14-18. Mark 9:14-27)

Jesus had just completed his mountaintop transfiguration experience where he communed with Elijah, Moses and God Himself. There he was, shining in all his glory in the presence of several disciples, receiving a reassuring voice from heaven. It was the utmost of spiritual experiences.

Then, a short time later, he found himself back in the physical realm with the crowds of people, the frustrations of life, and the vulnerability of being human. Instead of a reassuring voice from heaven, he heard a concerned father complaining about the lack of the disciples' ability to heal an illness. Instead of communing with God Almighty, he now confronted a demon infecting a child. Instead of the solitude and awesomeness of the mountaintop, he entered a valley of troubles.

Did you ever experience this type of contrast? One moment you're flying high, feeling the eternity of the moment, and soon you find yourself back into the challenges and tribulations of humanity. These are vicissitudes of life – the spiritual ecstasy versus the physical dangers of being human.

Even Jesus found this contrast frustrating. When the man approached Jesus complaining that the disciples could not heal his son, Jesus answered, "You faithless and perverse generation, how much longer must I be with you and bear with you?" Jesus's patience boiled over and he lashed out, not just at the father or the disciples, but at the situation he was facing. The clue to his reaction is actually found in verse 44: "Let these words sink into your ears; for the Son of Man is to be delivered into the hands of men." Jesus knew that his time on earth was short. The collective egos of this physical world carried no sense of love found in the spiritual world. He would soon be arrested and tried by those who felt threatened by his mission and message. He knew that it would lead to his execution.

Time was running out, and Jesus knew that he had to nurture his disciples to make sure that his mission and message carried on after he was gone. Were the disciples ready for the challenge? Did they really understand his message of love, compassion and mercy? Did they grasp the idea that if they worked together under this banner of love, that they could do many of the things that Jesus did – healing illnesses, expelling demons and changing people's hearts?

Despite his frustrations, Jesus stayed true to his mission of teaching and healing. "Jesus rebuked the unclean spirit, healed the boy, and gave him back to his father. And all were astounded at the greatness of God."

It's a good thing to remember: we *will* have ups and downs in life; we will have moments of spiritual ecstasy, and there will be times when we're not sure we can carry the burdens of being human. But what will pull us through those tough moments are the power and energy we receive from the mountaintop experiences. The more we can keep our eyes focused on our purpose in this life, the better we'll be able to weather the storms.

And we aren't supposed to do it alone, either. Jesus assembled a group of people around him for support and taught them how to help each other. No, they weren't perfect, but together their power and love was multiplied. We, too, need a spiritual support team close by that can truly get us through the rough times and can share the spiritual energy from the mountaintop times.

LUKE 9:43b-50

The Risk of Serving Others
(Matt. 17:22, 23; 18:1-5. Mark 9:30-40)

Jesus gently admonished his disciples when he heard them wondering who would be greatest in his kingdom. Their minds were still using a human system based on achievement and recognition, rather than one based on serving with love and compassion.

Jesus told them that in his kingdom, "Whoever wants to be first must be last of all and servant of all." He drilled this point home further by reminding them that it was not the rich and powerful that they necessarily should be serving – they may not be ready to receive any help – but the child, and people in need of care and attention. Once again, Jesus turned the rules of the world upside down. "Many that are first shall be last; and the last shall be first." (Matt. 19:30)

We shouldn't serve others in hopes of reaping some benefit, some attention, or some reward. We should serve others because it's the loving thing to do.

When our minds are on divine things, and not on human things, we begin to become better servants for God. And if we listen to our hearts carefully, we know that this yearning to serve God is one of our basic needs. We learn to become who God made us to be, with all our special interests, talents, abilities, and yes, even our faults, and that's the way we will serve Him best – in whatever life situation we find ourselves.

Being a servant of God, however, is not without risk. Jesus's message of love, compassion, and even economic equity among all peoples threatened the system of power and money being used at the time. People holding this power would seek to eliminate him.

A passage from the Wisdom of Solomon provides us with an understanding of why these people hated Jesus. "He is inconvenient to us and opposes our actions; he reproaches us for sins against the law...He professes to have knowledge of God, and calls himself a child of the Lord...His manner of life is unlike that of others, and his ways are strange." (Wisd. of Sol. 2:12-15)

Jesus knew he was upsetting the status quo. He knew he was hated and would be killed. He told his disciples, "The Son of

Man is to be betrayed into human hands, and they will kill him," but he added, "and three days after being killed, he will rise again." Even hatred could not stop God's plans.

Anyone who brings a message of love, compassion and mercy into this world places themselves at some risk. Simply by declaring yourself a Christian finds you some enemies. Living a life as a servant of God will create even more. It's part of the burden of carrying your cross.

So we have a conflict deep down inside of us – a tension between self-preservation as a physical human being and self-fulfillment as a child of God. God's tug at our heart also pushes against our basic needs of safety and security. The yearning He put into us to connect with other people and share His love sometimes clashes with our basic survival instinct, which can bully us into passivity and apathy.

Living a life of love can be dangerous, but there's no other way to really live. We lose everything physical at some point anyway, but we never lose what God gave us as His children. He proved His love for us through Jesus's death and resurrection. The love of God cannot be stopped by anything – even the death of His Son.

Know that you are loved, and you are not alone. God's love will prevail, and all will be made right. As the psalmist of Ps. 54 writes, "God is my helper; the Lord is the upholder of my life...for He has delivered me from every trouble."

LUKE 9:51-62

Living Love
(Matt. 8:19-22)

The currency of God is love. God is love itself. As Paul wrote in 1 Corinthians, "Love is patient, love is kind..." Love is not resentful, it doesn't seek revenge, it doesn't intentionally hurt us – it wants us to become fully, spiritually, human, and nothing will keep this from eventually happening. The fruits of love are joy, peace, patience, kindness, generosity, and gentleness.

If your image of God is anything else, think about changing it, because you're not realizing the full truth.

Love is also a choice *we* make. As was mentioned in previous segments, if it wasn't a choice, it wouldn't be love – it would be a software program. For us to be able to choose love, God had to take a risk and give us free will, the freedom to choose it.

Paul writes in his letter to the Galatians (5:13) that we are called to this freedom. We can choose to be a slave to our own egos (to become self-indulgent, as he calls it), or "become slaves to one another." He wasn't talking about a slavery of oppression, but a deep commitment of love for one another, in community (families, social groups, churches, support groups, etc.).

We don't lose our identity when we commit to a group through love; we actually enhance our identity through the interconnectedness that comes with a cohesive community. But pure individualism spawns social disintegration. Individualism can occur even when people interact on a daily basis with others at work or play, when that interaction is for a person's own benefit rather than for the benefit of the community.

Paul warns, "If you bite and devour one another, take care that you are not consumed by one another." (v. 15) It feels a little like this is what's happening in today's society.

The fruits of a life with the Spirit include "love, joy, peace, patience, kindness, generosity, faithfulness, gentleness, and self-control." (Gal. 5:22-23) These are nice things, indeed, but how does one live a life to get them? The secret is in the fruits of the Spirit themselves.

- *Love* your neighbors as yourself
- Be *joyful*
- Spread *peace*
- Be *patient*
- Show *kindness* to people, creatures, and the earth
- Be *generous* with your time, talent and treasures
- Share a smile and a blessing
- Have *faith* that all will be well
- Be *gentle* with others, and with yourself
- Be aware of each moment and how you are relating to it. What impact are you having right now, and how will it impact the future? This will help you with *self-control*.

The benefits of a life in the Spirit become the tools to get there; the tools bring the benefits. This is one of God's many circles of life that bring new life.

LUKE 10:1-20

The Challenge of Serving Others
(Matt. 11:20-24)

This section of Luke has value for us as we reach out to others in service, whether through an organized project, or simply in our moment-by-moment interaction as we move through the day.

We read that Jesus sent out seventy people (in some ancient sources it's seventy-two) on a mission to a number of cities to prepare the way for his future visits. Having been given the power to heal and preach the Good News, they eventually return to Jesus ecstatic about their success, "Lord, in your name even the demons submit to us!"

This news pleases Jesus greatly, but he also cautions them to keep things in perspective. Having this type of power and success can be a very tempting treat for the ego, leading to excessive self-pride that nurtures dysfunction. So, Jesus strikes an appropriate balance between honoring their victory and reminding them that it's more important to have their hearts and minds on the kingdom of God, "that your names are written in heaven."

The power they've been given to heal and preach the Gospel doesn't come from their own devices – it comes from God. All that we have in the way of talents, skills, abilities and interests are gifts from God, and are to be used to grow His kingdom of love, compassion and mercy in our own unique way, based on those gifts, wherever we have been planted on this earth. Our joy doesn't come from the things we possess, but by *being* possessed by God and His love.

Jesus reminds us, "The harvest is plentiful, but the laborers are few." And yet, if all people were able to discover and fully realize their true selves, appreciating and using in service whatever gifts they may have been given, the world would be a lot closer to becoming "heaven on earth." As more people awaken and expand their self-awareness, we get closer to this kingdom.

Being our true selves in the world is not always easy. Jesus warned the seventy that he was sending them out "like lambs into the midst of wolves." We won't always be accepted by others for who and what we have to offer. People who are trapped in their own dysfunctional egos, either individually or as a group, generally want to achieve their own objectives, and these goals may not be related to the goals of God's kingdom. If you are useful to these type of people in their pursuits, they will accept you, but only as long as they find value in you. If you can't be of use to them they will generally ignore you; if are a threat to their pursuits they may become your enemies.

But press forward anyway, Jesus encourages. Go where you are accepted, and do what you can there. If you're not accepted, go somewhere else and keep trying. But in every case, tell them that "the kingdom of God has come near you." In other words, regardless of who they are and what their state of mind might be, they are loved by God. All people are children of God, whether or not they are ready to awaken to His kingdom.

We have little idea how the things we do each moment impact other people; but each encounter is definitely a spiritual seed planted; some will fail to sprout, others will lay dormant for years, and some will begin to grow immediately. We've been asked to spread these seeds of love using our own gifts, talents and interests, serving God in our own unique way, moment by moment. This is our outer purpose in this world. The Holy Spirit will take it from there, and work Her magic in making things grow in the proper time and place.

LUKE 10:21-24

Discovered Truth and Revealed Truth
(Matt. 11:25-27; 13:16, 17)

As mankind moves through history, discoveries add to the understanding about the world, and make us feel more powerful and in control. We learn about gravity, the inertia of objects, the DNA building blocks of life, how particles behave, and how the weather works, to name a few.

Facts are discovered through careful observation, analysis and reason. As the extent of knowledge grows, so does our ability to grasp the complexities of life. Our pride in these accomplishments grows, creating a protective barrier around our discoveries which we then elevate to "truths." We begin to believe that we acquire secret pieces of the universe, and then go to great lengths to defend them from further skepticism and challenge.

History also shows that many of mankind's discovered "truths" tend to crack and crumble with age. The world isn't flat, stars are not pinholes in the celestial ceiling, and the earth is not the center of the universe. Even what we learn about people changes over time, too. We know, for example, that people are more similar in nature and structure with each other than we once thought. Race, ethnicity, age and gender are merely superficial differences that distract us from seeing the unity and interconnectedness among us all. We are indeed members of the same family, under one God.

I have learned to receive news of discoveries with cautious joy. What we learn as humans may indeed be facts, but these facts are highly conditional, and rarely merit the honor of being called a truth.

Revealed truths, on the other hand, are generally based on an absolute. They are usually broader in nature and don't really change over time, even though our understanding of them might. These types of truths are not discovered, but are offered to us as gifts. They don't come from the effort of the human mind, and only come to those ready and willing to receive them.

Jesus knew that the "wise and intelligent" (referring primarily to the scribes and Pharisees of his day) were so wrapped up in their own mental prowess that they would not be able to receive revealed truths. They placed their pride in what they acquired through their own effort. They did not have "eyes to see, or ears to hear." Over time, their pride fertilized the growth of dysfunctional egos which now ruled their thought and hardened their hearts.

Revealed truth has to do with the true nature of the universe, about God, and about His currency of love. We come to understand the inner beauty of the spirit, and how everything *is* really interconnected. We are all children of God, human beings made up of a physical part and a spiritual part, a unique blend of realms that is destined to further God's creation through the use of our own talents, skills, and abilities in the place that we've been planted, moment by moment.

Revealed truth is given to us when we position ourselves to receive it. A humble and contrite heart, a place of silence, a time of prayer, and vibrant awareness are the key ingredients. Jesus said to the disciples, "Blessed are the eyes that see what you see! For I tell you that many prophets and kings desired to see what you see, but did not see it, and to hear what you hear, but did not hear it."

LUKE 10:25-37

Mr. God's Neighborhood

A certain lawyer decided to test Jesus to see if Jesus even knew the basics of Judaic law. "What must I do to inherit eternal life?" asked the lawyer, knowing full well what the answer was. "Well, what is written in the law? What do you read there?" Jesus countered the question, putting the lawyer on the spot instead.

The response, of course, was what we know as the Great Commandment: "To love God ... and to love your neighbor as yourself." The lawyer wanted to repair his wounded ego after this rebuke by Jesus, so he intensified the challenge: "But who is my neighbor?" He hoped to back Jesus into a corner.

Jesus responded with a story, the well-known service of the Good Samaritan. Three people (a priest, a Levite, and a Samaritan) encounter a man who had been victimized by robbers. But it was only the Samaritan who stopped to help the poor man.

Initially, we might expect the definition of a neighbor to be about helping anyone in need, such as the man who was hurt by the robbers. Instead, the parable changes perspective and shows us what behaviors best exemplify that of a good neighbor – such as how the Samaritan offered his help.

Jesus's purpose in framing the story that way was to remind us that being a good neighbor is really a relationship, or perhaps a network of people helping others in a loving manner. In other words, it's really a "neighborhood."

Yes, it starts with someone who has some sort of need (which is just about everyone, isn't it?) but that need comes to our attention when we are willing to stay alert in the present moment and keep our eyes open.

Sometimes it's a big need, and quite obvious, like having been beaten by robbers; other times it's smaller, and may take a careful eye to discern, like the concerned look on another person's face, or someone who needs help with packages as they walk down the street.

The priest and the Levite refused to engage in a relationship with the robbed man – they chose to remain as isolated individuals, separating themselves from God, and themselves. Why did they ignore their brother in need? There are many possible excuses.

- Could be a trap; I'd better stay clear
- Someone else may retaliate against me
- Don't know how to help; may make things worse
- He's not one of us; not my concern (tribalism)
- No time; too busy right now
- The problem is too big; too far away, I'm powerless to do anything
- I was ordered by my superiors not to help
- It doesn't profit me to help those in need
- I really didn't see anything
- He got what he deserved – shouldn't have been there to get in trouble
- I don't have the resources to do any good

If we dig deep enough, most of these excuses, if not all, have their roots in fear: Fear that I may be hurt or lose something, fear that I may have to reveal something about myself to someone I don't want to. Fear that it will impact my life and change things I don't want changed.

Part of what fuels the fear of helping someone in need is that we often think that we have to resolve the issue on our own. The truth is, other than the little needs we come across, we usually don't have the power or resources to fully help someone else. Being a neighbor to someone in need is not just a one-on-one relationship. Even the Good Samaritan got others involved to help the man beaten by robbers. He brought the innkeeper into the neighborhood, and probably others helped the innkeeper at the inn.

Neighborhoods are not geographical locations, they're networks of people who are able to help each other in various ways. Each of us has been given some talents and gifts to contribute to the good of the world. No one person has it all. No one person can solve all the problems. But together we can. We've been designed to be part of God's neighborhood, not to be isolated individuals.

Stay alert for others' needs (and your own), moment by moment. But don't assume that when you run across something that you have to fix it all. Get the "neighborhood network" humming and work together on the issue as best you can. Eventually those with the ability and resources to help can get connected with those in need.

LUKE 10:38-42

Mary and Martha, Two Sides of Life

On some days I begin to feel somewhat unbalanced, somehow mentally lopsided. It can happen if I spend too much physical time working on a project, and I don't get some "down time" to relax and reflect. Or it can happen if I pass the day almost entirely in thought and reflection, not seeming to get anything else done. It's as if there were two different sides of me, each having to be satisfied.

I was reminded again of this needed action-contemplation balance in my life when I read the story of Mary and Martha. Martha shows me that there is an action-oriented side to life, the need to use whatever gifts I may have as an offering of service to others. She had the gift of hospitality; offering and preparing her home to make others feel welcomed, comfortable, and appreciated.

Mary, on the other hand, reminded me that there also is a passive, reflective side to life, a time to be quiet, a time to feed off the loving presence and words of God as they come to us through scripture, meditation, prayer, study, and reflection. To be of service to others, we must have something to offer, and much of the drive, desire, and energy to serve can come from our "down time." Mary took the opportunity of Jesus's presence by sitting at the Lord's feet to listen to what he had to say.

To be in balance, we must be presently aware of when we should be serving and when we should be praying. That's why we intersperse the work (service) with our prayers. We must feed all of these needs to be in balance.

For everything there is a season, and a time for every matter under heaven.
Ecclesiastes 3:1

Martha was right to invite Jesus into her home. She went wrong, however, when she mixed up her time of service with her time to listen. Once Jesus was in her home, it was obviously a time to listen and learn. But Luke reports that she "was distracted by her many tasks." Her need for action interfered with contemplative time. She even tried to interfere with Mary's time of contemplation. Martha asked Jesus to "tell Mary to help me." In other words, Mary should stop listening to Jesus and get busy.

Jesus pointed out that what Mary was doing was the best thing at this moment. We know that people "can't live by bread alone, but by every word that comes from the mouth of God." (Matt. 4:4) To properly serve others at the proper time, we need the wisdom and encouragement to do it. *Without a proper purpose for our service work, we lose focus and can get easily distracted by many unimportant things.* God-time gives us the power and direction for action-time. And then, in turn, our action-time will enrich our God-time.

Eventually, this action-contemplation rhythm blends together into the heartbeat of each moment. We constantly feel the presence of God providing us with guidance, encouragement, reassurances, love and rest, which is the deep meaning of "pray always." And we are also constantly on the look-out for ways to interact with others, moment by moment, using whatever skills, abilities, and kindnesses we've been given to offer to others in the spirit of unity with the human family.

For me, it's the blend of action and contemplation (Martha and Mary) that make me whole – filling me with the natural love of God, allowing me to share that love with others moment by moment.

LUKE 11:1-13

Teach Us to Pray
(Matt. 6:9-13; 7:7-11)

The disciples kept seeing Jesus going off to some quiet place to pray, usually alone, at almost any time of the day or night. They wondered about it; they knew it was important to Jesus, and their interest gradually piqued to a point where they wanted to know more about it: "Lord, teach us to pray."

As I was growing up, I used to see my mother praying; sometimes kneeling at her bed, sometimes sitting in a chair, sometimes with a pen in hand creating a note of wisdom or guidance that would be taped to the wall of our bedroom. Like the disciples, it made me curious about what prayer was all about, and gradually I began to explore prayer, too.

Jesus captured this teachable moment in Luke 11 by not only teaching the disciples *what* things to say in prayer, but also *how* and *why* to pray. He began by giving them the now-famous Lord's Prayer (the more common version is found in Matthew's record). It immediately set the tone for what prayer is all about – emphasizing the unity of God with all of His children – "Our Father..." Everyone is part of God's family; we're all connected in one way or another through our relationship with God, our Father. God unites, evil divides.

"Your Kingdom come..." Jesus reminds us that the main purpose for our prayers is to unite God's Kingdom with our lives, not only at some point in the future when Jesus returns to Earth via the "Second Coming," but right now, right here, in our very own hearts and minds. Jesus frequently reminds us that the Kingdom of God is actually already here, surrounding us, and within us. All we have to do is open our hearts and minds to receive it.

The purpose of praying is to dissolve the things surrounding our hearts that are blocking us from receiving the Kingdom right now. Prayer is not just about reciting words from a book, getting to the end, and feeling that we have accomplished something. Prayer is a tool for *changing the state of our minds* to become channels for feeling the Presence of God, receiving the power of His love for us and the world, and turning this transformation into action for ourselves and others. We might reach this point early in a prayer session, or later. When this channel is opened, we can listen, learn, ask, and grow in His love.

"Our daily bread..." Jesus taught that people can't live by bread alone, but by every word that comes from the mouth of God. Our daily bread is not only the basic nutritional sustenance that we all need, but also the daily *spiritual* sustenance that we all need – nurturing by the Presence of the Holy Spirit in our hearts, meeting us at our point of need, moment by moment. Our daily bread is no more, or no less, than what it takes to fully live each and every moment.

"Forgive us our sins..." Forgiveness is of utmost importance – not only of others, but of ourselves as well. We all have a "shadow side," the accumulation of mistakes, malice and misplaced desires from our past. It also includes the potential for making mistakes in the future. It means we're human, but that doesn't diminish God's love for us. The imperfections of our shadow side result in gaps and potholes that God loves to fill in with His love. Yes, sometimes this process can be painful, but it moves us toward His perfection. Acceptance and forgiveness of ourselves and others makes filling the holes possible.

"Save us from the time of trial." Lead us not into temptation – We ask for the Presence of God's Holy Spirit to guide us and direct us, giving us the wisdom and strength to remember that we are a child of God seeking to do His will each and every moment of the day.

Jesus went on to stress that persistence in prayer was important, too. His story about the midnight friend in this segment of Luke was not meant to mean that we must be persistent to awaken a sleeping God, but that persistence in prayer was important to awaken ourselves. We often need persistence to overcome the fetters created by a dysfunctional ego – our own self-pride, arrogance, boredom, or indifference. The struggle with prayer is usually with ourselves, not with God.

Our Father will give us the "good gifts," the things we really need in this life to become who we were made to be. It may not always move as fast as we like, or come in the manner we expected, but His plans for us will come to pass regardless.

Eventually as we progress on our spiritual journey, we begin to "pray always" as Paul wrote. (1 Thes. 5:17) This means we always are in the proper state of mind to receive and share God's love, regardless of where we are or what we are doing. Prayer blends into service, and service blends into prayer. Our study blends into prayer, and leads to better service. Our service gives us more to study.

To learn to pray is to learn to live.

LUKE 11:14-28

The Great Void
(Matt. 12:22-30, 43-45. Mark 3:20-27)

The wealth of this lesson can be summed up in a quote from St. Augustine in his *Confessions*, "You have made us for yourself, O Lord, and our heart is restless until it rests in you." People are designed to be interconnected with God. Every moment of our life was meant to be based on the love of God – every thought, every word, every deed. It's a companionship that was indeed made in heaven.

But God won't force us into this relationship. Since this relationship is based on love, and love has to be a choice, this relationship with God also has to be a choice. He has given us free will to choose our way.

A life of unity with God sometimes takes a lifetime to achieve. We are pulled and pushed in many directions as we grow up and move through time. Many influences shape our lives, including social, cultural, genetic, political or educational forces, to name a few. Not all of them support building a harmonic relationship with God.

Whenever God is absent, a void develops that cries to be filled. Nature abhors a vacuum, and does what it can to fill it in. The same thing happens with your spiritual bearing. If something comes along that *seems* to fill the void, it'll be adopted and made part of a person's identity. Sometimes the person chooses an escape activity; sometimes they fall victim to dysfunctional ego development by identifying with material things, thoughts, ideas, or situations. They become obsessed with power, greed, lust, popularity, money, food, or drugs.

The dysfunctional ego goes to great lengths to preserve and defend itself. It becomes so identified with its thoughts and ideas that it will attack any threat to it. This is why the people in this story attacked Jesus – because his power to heal threatened them.

"He is using power from Beelzebul!" some charged. Others demanded a sign from heaven to prove Jesus got his power from God (not realizing, of course, that the healing itself was a sign from heaven). The ego feels stronger if it can diminish the stature and character of another person. The ego feels better if it can feel superior. How much of this goes on today? Too much!

Spiritual voids must be filled with the Presence of God or something else might try to fill the gap. When someone has been healed of an illness, particularly one related to a psychological issue, the void left by the healing must be replaced with something better. Jesus explained that the expelled "demon" returns to a person to find an empty house, now put in order, and waiting for occupancy. So, the demon goes and gets seven more demons to fill the welcoming void there.

What's the lesson in this for us? Part of any healing process must include filling all the empty spaces with the Presence of God. To be freed from the power of a problem is not enough; a higher power must be put in its place or the dysfunction may return, ever stronger. Where can we get this higher power? Through a structured practice that consists of some combination of therapy, counseling, prayer, meditation, contemplation, walks in nature, lectio divina, journaling, reflective study, discussions with friends and spiritual directors, and service to others – anything that promotes and sustains the love of God within the person.

LUKE 11:29-36

The Sign of Jonah
(Matt. 5:15; 6:22, 23; 12:38-42. Mark 8:12)

Ignoring the fact that Jesus's healing powers themselves could be considered a sign from God, many of the people of his time still demanded a heavenly sign that Jesus had been given authority from God. But Jesus knew that these people were so imprisoned by their own dysfunctional egos that they wouldn't believe in him regardless of what he did or said. So, he confronted them, saying that they would get no sign, except for the sign of Jonah.

But what was this sign of Jonah?

One of the most well-known stories of the Hebrew Scriptures, Jonah spent three days in the belly of a great fish because he didn't want to obey God. Some say the sign of Jonah is the fact that Jesus, like Jonah, was gone after the crucifixion, and then returned – Jonah being "spewed forth" by the great fish, and Jesus being resurrected from the dead.

The resurrection of Jesus is indeed one of the most important cornerstones of Christianity. It affirmed that nothing, not even the murder of God's only begotten Son, could come between God and His love for us. Paul emphasized this in his letter to the Romans when he wrote, "For I am convinced that neither life, nor death, nor angels, nor principalities, nor powers, nor things present, nor things to come, nor height, nor depth, nor any creature, shall be able to separate us from the love of God, which is in Jesus Christ our Lord." (Rom. 8:38-39) God's love is unconditional and eternally steadfast.

But was the resurrection supposed to be the sign of Jonah? Consider that Jonah was held captive because of his disobedience to God, but Jesus was murdered because of his *obedience* to God. Jonah did not die from his great fish experience, but Jesus did die. And while Jonah was alone in the belly of the great fish, Jesus was able to visit some lost souls in hell and free them from their bonds. So, there might be enough differences to explore other possibilities.

Some commentators suggest that the sign of Jonah was the Jesus's preaching itself. Both Jesus and Jonah delivered a message of repentance to a lost people. Preaching the Word of God has been equated to being a miracle in itself, as suggested by Paul: "For I am not ashamed of the gospel of Christ: For it is the power of God unto salvation to everyone that believes…" (Rom. 1:16) and "…your faith should not stand in the wisdom of men, but in the power of God." (1 Cor. 2:5) The Word of God carries a lot of power, and has changed many lives.

Perhaps this is the sign: that some people are actually changed for the better if they actually accept the Word and are transformed by it. When Jonah preached his message to the people, they repented and changed the way they were living. "The people of Nineveh believed God, and they proclaimed a fast, and put on sackcloth, from the greatest of them even to the least of them." (Jonah 3:5)

The true miracle, the whole purpose of the gospel, is to have people return willingly to God's care and guidance. The sign of Jonah may not be as much the preaching as it is *the result* of the preaching. For those with eyes to see, and ears willing to hear, the wisdom of God does indeed change the lives of people – and that is truly a powerful sign. If the Word is true, if Jesus did in fact have God's authority, then people could change if they listened to and accepted his teaching.

The last four verses of this passage in Luke lend support to this idea. "Lighting a lamp" is a metaphor for someone who has been enlightened by the Word of God. People who change have been shown their true selves, their own soul, and are now aware of the truth about life. (It doesn't mean they're perfect, but that they've begun the journey back home to God.)

The "eye" is the portal of understanding and compassion. It is the present moment awareness of God's Presence in life, in and around each of us. If the eye is not clouded with a dysfunctional ego or troubled spirit, it will let in more light. This light is a gift from God, ever-present and available to us – the Kingdom of God is at hand!

LUKE 11:37-54

The Inside of the Cup
(Matt. 23:1-36; Mark 12:38-40)

Jesus criticizes both the Pharisees and the scribes in this segment of Luke. But rather than attacking a specific group of people, Jesus's intent was to highlight some of the more common pitfalls of people running institutions like religious organizations. He specifically targets externalism, legalistic pedantry, religious ostentation, and pious hypocrisy. These problems can easily infect our leaders of today, too.

The problem starts when people pay more attention to what can be physically seen than what is spiritually important. In religious practices, ritualism can grow so that each movement and rubric is performed correctly at the expense of the needs of worshipers. It involves creating an outward appearance of piety when the internal proceedings fall short of graciousness and compassion. It involves claiming that salvation depends on rules and expectations, but fails to consider the pressures and situation of those struggling in life.

But what is the root problem? It's in the chasm between the outward public image created by those in leadership and the true self of their souls on the inside. Their growing dysfunctional collective egos create an outward illusion that is fed by their power and authority. Their outward appearance is highly polished because they "clean the outside of the cup and of the dish," but they neglect the more important soul that gradually gets covered over by layers of "greed and wickedness."

If we lose the bearing on our soul, on the spiritual intent of life itself, either on an individual basis, or as leaders on a collective basis, then the individual or the organization slowly decays. It's eventually replaced by new hope, new direction, and new leadership.

Part of every organization, or each person's life for that matter, should include a periodic check on the cleanliness of the "inside." Is the love of God still in view or is something else obstructing the way? Is something that's supposed to help in the mission of God now become the thing worshipped? People must practice the discernment of spirits to keep on track. Look for signs that things aren't going well, and then raise the red flag of warning.

LUKE 12:1-12

The Unforgivable Sin
(Matt. 10:28-33; 12:32)

The crowd gathered once again to listen to Jesus, but before he spoke to them he had some words of guidance for his disciples. He got right to the core issue of humanity, which he called the leaven, or yeast, of the Pharisees. The issue wasn't exclusive to Pharisees, but the Pharisees (at least some of them) served as a good example of what he was talking about.

What was this leaven? He called it their *hypocrisy*. This wasn't so much a case of the Pharisees saying one thing and doing another (the usually understanding of hypocrisy), as it was a case of them *being* one thing (that was false) when they were really something else deep down inside (their true self).

The Merriam-Webster dictionary defines hypocrisy as "feigning to be what one is not or feigning to believe what one does not." The word is derived from the roles that people would play on a stage – interacting with others based on a false image being.

In other words, it's the refusal to be who we were made to be, feigning to be someone else – driven by a dysfunctional ego that pursues and strives for the things of mankind's world instead of God's world. If we think about it, this may be the root cause of most, if not all, of our troubles in this world. People fight people, groups fight groups, and nations fight nations, all because we've lost our sense of connection with each other as children of the One God. We abandon our true selves, our souls, to the devices and desires of illusion. A higher unifying principle is lost, and we latch onto provincial ideals for survival based on fear of the unknown. Our ignorance grows deeper the more we fortify our public image with power, avarice, prejudice, wealth, or superiority.

Jesus knew that if we really got in touch with our true selves, we would realize the kingdom of God within us. The truth is basic to any understanding of community, any hope of peace, or any possibility of joy. Jesus warned against hypocrisy more than anything else because it was the great barrier that prevented true fellowship. It begins with a deception of oneself and then tries to deceive others. It isn't based on love, but rather on fear.

Jesus continues to teach his disciples that eventually "nothing is covered up that will not be uncovered." In the kingdom of God, all truth will be known – false barriers will dissolve, and people will be seen for who they truly are. This is not a bad thing, because God's eternal kingdom will be built on a love of truth. When people are relieved of the heavy burden of their false selves, they will weep for joy. Some may continue to resist for a while, "gnashing their teeth" at the thought of letting go their tight identities with illusion. But eventually their individualism will melt into the bonds of community where they will be made whole.

Yes, God has the power to do what He wants – and for this we should be in *awe* of Him (the true meaning of "fear" in this case). But we also learn from verse 7 that we shouldn't be afraid of Him, because He values us simply as an object of His love – not because we may have been "great" in our earthly life.

When we refuse to truly know ourselves (this refusal is of our own free will) preferring instead to live a false life, then we have effectively shut out the Grace of God in our lives. This is the "blasphemy against the Holy Spirit," who guides and sustains our lives here on Earth. The Holy Spirit is our

Advocate and Teacher in life, the active link we have with God's Grace. This deliberate choice to block out this Grace might make it impossible for the repentance and forgiveness needed to reestablish the connections with the kingdom. It is unforgivable not so much because God won't do it, but because we won't let Him. The problem is in *our* hypocrisy – *our* hardness of heart.

We must work to discover our true selves, the connections we have with each other as brothers and sisters, and the connections we have with this planet and all the creatures upon it. Develop the disciplines of daily prayer, reflective study, and serving others in the spirit of unity, respect and peace. Eventually, your true self will emerge and you will enjoy the fruits of the Holy Spirit.

LUKE 12:13-21
Greed is Good...Not!

Jesus takes on the problem of greed in Luke 12. He warns, "Take care! Be on your guard against all kinds of greed; for one's life does not consist in the abundance of possessions."

On the other hand, "Greed is good," exclaims Gordon Gekko in the 1987 movie *Wall Street*. "Greed works. Greed clarifies, cuts through, and captures the essence of the evolutionary spirit. Greed, in all of its forms – greed for life, for money, for love, for knowledge – has marked the upward surge of mankind."

And so we have the classic wisdom versus the world's viewpoints, leaving mankind in the swirl of a lifelong struggle.

One of the underlying challenges for us is that we're part physical being and part spiritual being. Together, they make us a human being. The physical part has been hardwired for survival and security. The world is a dangerous place, and certainly not always fair. Many of us have experienced the impact of a flawed economic system that cares little about individuals. The world Gordon Gekko praises is one that creates inequality which benefits some people while harming others – it's survival of the "fittest."

So, one of our basic drives is to secure enough "stuff" to make sure that we *can* survive and prosper in a tough world. We don't trust the system, and we feel like we're in the race for ourselves. The present system is uncertain and unforgiving. It fails many people.

Why do we build such an unstable system using our own principles and laws? Because we really don't trust the wisdom of God. And this isn't a new problem – Hosea speaks of it when he reports what God said: "The more I called [my people], the more they went from me ... My people are bent on turning away from me." (Hosea 11:2, 7)

Why don't the people trust God? Usually when we don't trust people it's because we don't really know them. Same with God, I suppose. We don't always trust Him because we don't really know Him very well. We hear conflicting reports from various groups about what God stands for, and it leaves us confused. We often listen to other people about who and what God is, and it always seems to leave us incomplete.

Why don't people really know God? When we really want to know what another person is like, we must spend time with that other person, and not listen to what other people say about that person. We need to experience that person ourselves. It's the same with God. We don't really know God because we don't really spend enough time with Him in prayer, meditation, contemplation, nature, and finding Him in other people.

Why don't we spend enough time with God? One of the reasons, which Jesus pointed out at the very beginning of this lesson, is that we're too busy striving for survival and security – and that leaves little room for God. In Ecclesiastes we read, "Vanity of vanities, all is vanity! (v. 1:2) ... It is an unhappy business for mankind to be too busy (v.1:13) ... for their days are full of pain, and their work is a vexation – even at night their minds do not rest." (v. 2:23)

Jesus did not say it was wrong to work or have possessions. What he was stressing was that when the physical human needs dominate one's time and effort, then the spiritual being needs suffer. If we gain a good balance, our heads will clear, and we will be able to do many things the right way, including developing an economic system using God's wisdom that leaves no one behind.

Greed and hoarding will no longer be necessary in God's kingdom. And, contrary to what Gordon Gekko believes, humans will continue to evolve into the human beings they were meant to be, building a society based on wisdom, love and community that far outshines what we have today.

LUKE 12:22-31

In God We Trust
(Matt. 6:25-34)

The inscription "In God We Trust" is on almost every piece of money in the United States. It's logical to assume that those words are there to remind us that we trust in God. But I'm not so sure we really know what that means – at least I don't often see it happening.

Jesus took an opportunity in Luke 12 to further instruct his disciples about trusting God. We take these words today as instruction about the faithfulness of God to us: Don't worry about what you will eat or what you will wear, because God loves you more than the birds, and more than the lilies, and He takes care of them, right? So He will take care of you, too.

Really? But wait a minute – what about all the people who die of starvation each year, or suffer from exposure to the cold for lack of proper clothing? What about all the homeless people in this land of plenty; the ever-flowing amber waves of grain? What about the animals who starve, and the millions of birds who die each year by smashing into windows? And the honey bees, and the polar bears, and the whales... The world is really a mess!

On the surface, it appears that these claims by Jesus are rather absurd. If the current world we have is a result of our trust in God, then something is definitely amiss.

Perhaps the key to this puzzle is found in the last verse of this Gospel segment: "Strive for His kingdom and these things will be given to you as well." Ah! The results of trusting in God appear to be based on our *striving for His kingdom.* The nations of the world, however, strive after all the material needs in life, and the result is worry, stress, and anxiety. But God says to pursue His kingdom first, and all these other material things would be provided – stress-free, worry-free, and without anxiety. This is not happening now, because we really don't trust the idea that if we pursue God's kingdom first, we would really get these good things. We put more trust in a system we've been using for centuries, a system that we created using our own rules that we're most familiar with despite its shortcomings. It's the best system we know.

Therein we find the issue: Maybe it's too much of a risk for most of us, especially all of us as a nation (much less the world as a whole) to believe that if we lived according to the kingdom of God we would no longer have to strive for the necessities of life, and that all our stress, worry, and anxiety would vanish. And we really don't know *how* to strive for the kingdom of God even if we actually believed it *would* work.

We don't know how to translate the wisdom of Jesus into economic or governance principles that would actually work for the benefit of the all while still preserving the uniqueness of the individual. Those with an excessive amount of material wealth might oppose such a system that may topple their power structure, just as they opposed it in Jesus's day. We are uncertain about the changes that such a system would bring, or if it really would bring peace and harmony to the world. It just seems so out of reach – Fantasyland!

Maybe before we can all agree that we need a better system, we'll have to continue with what we have until we're fed up with its flaws. Maybe mankind must try every conceivable form of government and social structure before there is nothing left to try – except the kingdom. This realization could be many years away, if we don't destroy ourselves first.

If we do finally get to that turning point, we'll need people to study the Scriptures, to scan the piles of reflective writings by the great mystics and philosophers, to gather together in regular prayer and discernment, and to make changes in the world based on God's love, compassion and mercy. We'll really need to understand mankind's psyche, and be able to unlock important areas of the collective unconscious, revealing the extensive interconnections we have with one another, with God, and with the planet itself.

It'll be a much different world than the world we live in today – it will be like heaven on Earth! Besides the reminder on our coins to trust in God might be the active prayer, "Thy kingdom come, Thy will be done, on Earth as it is in heaven."

LUKE 12:32-34

The Physical and Spiritual Worlds
(Matt. 6:19-21)

"It is your Father's good pleasure to give you the kingdom," Jesus teaches. This is perhaps one of the most positive and hopeful revelations about God and His love for us. What greater gift could we possibly ever get?

We have learned in earlier passages what the kingdom of God is like. Almost beyond description, it contains the essence of everything for which our souls desire. The eternal company of God in all His glory, where there are no more tears of sorrow, no more pain, and where there is a full knowledge of our place and belonging within the Holy Realm. There we are complete, but continue in the growth and love of God, exploring the cosmos and gaining deeper understanding of life and love in all its varieties and interconnectedness. The fruit of the Holy Spirit flows continuously through all the creatures and elements.

But Jesus was quite clear that this gift is not only part of the future, it's also accessible, to a great degree, in our present lives as well. We open the portals of heaven on Earth when we rest in the present moment, shedding all our baggage from the past, and dropping all our fears and worries about the future. We become aware of our surroundings, and the reality of place. We begin to see people and things deeply, how everything is interconnected, and how we are all brothers and sisters in One Family, under God. We see a world of abundance, not scarcity, and we begin to realize the potential in the diversity of the people and the world. As we become aware of this, our illusions and mental infirmities dissolve like the scales from Paul's eyes after his road to Damascus experience.

"Sell your possessions," Jesus advised. Here Jesus was after something much deeper than merely getting rid of your things. By "sell your possessions," he meant relinquishing the emotional and egoistic attachments we have to things that often become more important to us than the relationships with other people and the planet itself. We mask the eternal riches of the kingdom when we focus on the temporary riches of our earthly things. You'll soon discover that you don't need as much as you thought you did, and there will be excess that can be used to help those in need.

"Purses wear out," "thieves can steal," and "moths destroy," warns Jesus about the material things we try so hard to hold on to. We live in two worlds – a physical world where all things are subject to constant change, and a spiritual world where the things of value are eternally safe and secure. Everything in the physical world *will change*. Nothing stays the same; things come and go, they wear out, they rot, they die. As soon as we can fully recognize and accept this fact, we will gain great mental and emotional health. Why? Because then we can begin to better recognize the spiritual world in and around us – this is where we must place our attachments and connections – our treasures!

We are spiritual beings living in a physical world. But too often the physical world captures the bulk of our attention and focus. Too often we spend our time seeking, accumulating, and protecting material things, and it costs us the priceless awareness of everything spiritual. Certainly, we need those material things to survive and grow in this world. Jesus had no problem with that – he used material things, too! But his warning was not to let those things get in the way of our true selves, our souls, because "where your treasure is, there your heart will be also."

LUKE 12:35-48

The Inner and Outer Kingdoms
(Matt. 24:45-51)

The early Christians anticipated Christ's return to Earth within a short time after his ascension. Their minds were filled with images of a new world order, a new government, and a new sense of peace. It seemed that Jesus spoke of this many times, like his affirmation in Luke 12, "Do not be afraid, little flock, for it is your Father's good pleasure to give you the

Kingdom." These people had faith that this new kingdom would come soon, whose "architect and builder is God." (Heb. 11)

A new heaven and a new earth will be upon us someday. But the expectations of the early Christians regarding a new physical kingdom here on Earth have yet to be realized. We can readily see that humankind suffers under the dominion of pervasive forces, and has so suffered for millennia. True peace, safety, equality, and justice still elude us.

And yet, it's also apparent to me that the Kingdom of God is all around us, and in us, wherever we turn, just waiting for us to say, "Yes, come in ... Come in to our lives and show us the way." It's as though all we have to do is walk into that room, that holy chamber of our soul, and flip the switch to "on."

This is the *inner* Kingdom of God that Jesus spoke most often about. It's already here, present to us, in the present moment, if we could only keep our dysfunctional ego from blocking it. God wants us to have it, and to have it now – not at some distant point in the far-off future.

"The Kingdom of God is within you," Jesus declares in Luke 17. "The Kingdom of God is at hand," he asserts in Matt. 10. This inner Kingdom of God is the place we must start if we want to bring the outer Kingdom of God to us. It's an inside-out proposition.

The inner Kingdom of God happens when we open ourselves up to the wisdom and teaching of Jesus, learn it, and apply it to our lives. It's the wisdom and love found not only in the Gospels, but also from the teachings of the Advocate he gave to us in our hearts: "And I will ask the Father, and he will give you another Advocate, to be with you forever. This is the Spirit of truth, whom the world cannot receive, because it neither sees him nor knows him. You know him, because he abides with you, and he will be in you." (John 14)

Listening, believing, applying, and practicing the wisdom and love of God will bring the inner Kingdom of God to us, which will eventually lead us to the outer Kingdom of God. By opening up to, and accepting this wisdom and love, we'll begin to find a balance in our own lives – between our mind, body and spirit – that brings an inner peace.

This inner peace will work its way out to people around us, building solid relationships based on the love and wisdom of God. And, over time, this will begin to change our culture and society itself. Eventually, we'll find ourselves in a new heaven and a new earth.

But we must never forget the living glue that holds all this together is the continued Presence of God in our lives. Without this Presence, the balance in our lives begins to crumble, and we lose sight of the vision. There is no perfection without the continued Presence of God. It was designed this way to keep us always together, and should never be forgotten.

That is why we build our lives around prayer and meditation, study and reflection, and service to others – to open ourselves up to this inner Kingdom of God, thank God for it, adopt it, practice it, and use it in our lives. For us, it's not a destination, but a continuous journey of learning – of falling down and getting back up, of trial and error, of mistakes and forgiveness.

LUKE 12:49-59

A Radical Wisdom
(Matt. 5:25-26; 10:34-36; 16:2-3)

Choosing a Christian life doesn't mean that we will be immune to conflicts in our own lives. In fact, Jesus makes it a point in Luke 12 that it's likely the opposite may happen.

The great peacemaker, Jesus himself, exclaims, "Do you think that I have come to bring peace to the earth? No, I tell you, but rather division!" He went on to describe how members of a family may be sharply divided because of his teachings.

We must be clear that it isn't Jesus's intent to cause trouble between family members, or between people within a society. Actually, he wants peace and harmony not only in families, but throughout the world. But he also knows that the message he brings, the wisdom he offers about how we should be living together and treating each other, will bring joy to some, and fear to others.

The wisdom that Jesus teaches is radical. And by radical I mean that it's so different from the way people normally live that it will either be embraced as something wonderful because of the change it offers, or it will be viciously attacked because of the change it threatens. It all depends on perspective, and that's what causes the division.

Jesus taught that there should be equality and unity among people; that we're all in the same family of God; God is our Parent, and we are all his children. This doesn't sit well with racists, bigots, or chauvinists.

Jesus promoted an economic system that provided the basic food, clothing and shelter to *every* person who is incapable of working, or who is willing to work, but can't find work. This doesn't sit well with those who cringe at the thought of somebody getting something for nothing.

Jesus taught us to be honest and fair with everyone. But this doesn't sit well with those who bend the rules a little here and a little there to increase profits, sometimes at the expense and health of consumers.

Jesus taught us to respect nature and all of God's creation. But this doesn't sit well with those who can make a profit at the expense of our food, air, water, soil, and wildlife.

Jesus taught us that the worth of a person should be determined by what's in his or her heart, not by how big their house is, or what kind of car they're driving, or if they're physically attractive. This doesn't sit well with advertisers and product developers who depend on creating desires where they don't exist naturally.

Jesus taught us to love our neighbor. What!? Even if that neighbor has a different belief about God? Even if they don't pay their employees fairly? Even if they make way too much money? Even if they're racists? Or bigots? Even if they're homeless? Even if they're lazy?

Yes.

Jesus's wisdom is radical because it challenges us to love our neighbors at the same time we work to bring more of God's loving ways to this earth. Yes, there should be peace and harmony among all people, and with the earth. But, yes, our activism will also bring conflict because it challenges old norms and standards. Some will like this, and some won't.

Even those with who we're in conflict should be treated as children of God, and with respect and reverence, says Jesus. We should also seek to be conciliatory, if possible, while we work toward our goals with gentle assertiveness. But we don't compromise on God's love.

Each one of us plays a significant role in God's overall plan. Each one of us has been given some special gifts that come into play at specific moments during the day. It may be just a well-placed blessing, a smile, a word of appreciation, a few minutes of listening, a helping hand, creating a piece of art, or simple admiration of God's creation. These things may not seem big to us, but they are huge to God.

We all have something to offer. Together, collectively as God's children, we bring the love into this world that is so desperately needed – resulting, perhaps, in a new heaven and a new Earth.

LUKE 13:1-9
Not to Condemn, But to Save

Some commentators on Luke 13 believe that this passage alludes to what is commonly referred to as the "Day of Judgment." Perhaps this position is based on the repeated phrases in Luke which read, "...but unless you repent, you will all perish as they did."

There is a natural desire to want ultimate justice. The good guy wins the battle and reaps the rewards, and the bad guy is duly and severely punished. Many of our cowboy westerns and modern day action films are based on this model. After all, it seems only fair. So when we read such verses, it's easy to assume that there must be a heavenly system that will uphold our human concept of justice, sending good souls to eternal bliss, and bad souls to eternal damnation.

God's system of justice, however, may have a far different objective. Instead of separating the "good guys from the bad guys," He is more interested in separating our good self from the bad self. In other words, the focus is to restore each and every person to wholeness, removing those things that are not of God, so that what remains is what was intended to be. It's spiritual surgery at its finest.

When Jesus warned his listeners that "...unless you repent, you will all perish as they did," he may have been describing what we *do to ourselves* when we're separate from God, rather than what God would do *to* us as punishment. The symbolism found in the story of the Exodus supports the idea that God's love for us is unconditional, and that He will work with us to remove the things that oppress us and keep us from His grace.

The Exodus reminds us of how God had "seen the affliction of [His] people in Egypt, and have heard their cry..." (v. 3:7) Clearly God knows the people's sorrows and sets in motion plans to help them through Moses. The oppressors of the Hebrews in Egypt kept them in physical bondage, but the symbolism of the story could include any oppression that diminishes our own souls, particularly the impact of a misguided, dysfunctional ego.

God frequently works through other people to help those in need. Moses was His instrument of choice for the Exodus from Egypt. Today, "Moses" may be those people who help us on our own spiritual journey. The Exodus journey for us is our journey back to wholeness. It may be a long journey through a wilderness that seems to have no end. For some, it may even be a 40-year trek through a dry desert with stony paths.

But along the way, we gradually begin to understand that God is trying to show us how to get rid of the things in us that are not of Him, so that what's left is pure and good. It's not a test to see if we qualify as "good" or "bad" as a person, but to recognize that there is good and bad mixed together, and we must sort it out with His help.

That's what happened to the people during the Exodus. They had to learn what worked, and what didn't. If they went too far away from God, they generally imploded – they self-destructed. This story is repeated many times in history – people or nations who turn their backs on the love, compassion and mercy of God will eventually collapse under the pressure of illusion and deception. Accurate translations of scripture don't say that God destroys these people, but that they end up destroying themselves.

Paul writes to the Corinthians that many people of the Exodus displeased God, "and they were struck down in the wilderness." (1 Cor. 10:5) They were not struck down by God, but decayed from the inside out. They fell to idolatry, immorality, bickering, doubt, and lack of contentment. They gave up their higher standards of love, unity, community, family, purpose and direction, only to settle for selfishness, illusion, and idolatry. Individuals, and societies, can't survive in this state. By the time the people reached the Promised Land, they learned many lessons.

Anyone's spiritual journey can be challenging. So we shouldn't expect the journey to be easy. But the extent of God's love for us makes it impossible for Him to give up on us. It just can't happen!

So Jesus's warnings in Luke to repent were pleas to choose a life following God, or we may risk losing the richness such a life offers. He does not want us to lose these spiritual gifts. Let Him "dig around your roots," to nurture you and help you grow – to bear fruit of His love, compassion and mercy.

LUKE 13:10-17

The Sacred Sabbath

The origin of the seven-day week and the Sabbath day tradition began in Genesis 2: "And on the seventh day God ended His work which He had done, and He rested. Then God blessed the seventh day and sanctified it, because in it He rested from all His work which He had created and made."

The importance of this seventh day of rest (Hebrew *shabbot*, meaning to cease, desist, and rest) elevated it to one of the Ten Commandments brought down from Mt. Sinai by Moses: "Remember the Sabbath day to keep it holy..." (Exod. 20:8-11) It became a foundational piece in Judaic culture, playing an important part in many other books of Hebrew scripture. It even played a central role in the Gospels and the growth of the new Christian church.

Like many of God's early guideposts given to help a youthful nation to mature, the Sabbath gradually became encrusted with specific rituals and laws about what could and couldn't be done on that day. It even got to the point that infractions of some of these rules could be punished by death!

People thought very strict obedience to specific rules was the way to God. (We see this yet today in some social and religious groups.) Over time, the reasons for having the Sabbath in the first place became obscured – lost in a maze of rituals and regulations.

But Jesus reminded us, "The Sabbath was made for people, and not the people for the Sabbath." (Mark 2:27) God created the Sabbath for mankind's benefit – not for his own.

We live in a busy world; our lives are full of busy-ness, largely about things of this world. The busier we are, the easier it can be to lose track of who we really are, where we came from, and where we're ultimately going in the long run. We get disconnected from God as we get immersed in worldly things.

God knew this could happen, and He knew how to keep us connected with Him. One day each week, He counseled, we are to set aside our worldly interests and instead spend time getting reacquainted with Him. It's part of the universal rhythm of activity and rest so that we can recharge our spiritual batteries, reset our moral compass, and reaffirm God's love for each of us.

How do we "remember the Sabbath to keep it holy?" By being with God. We can do this by attending worship services, taking walks in nature, being with family and friends, spending time helping someone else, reading about Him, praying with Him, and thanking Him. Psalm 103 reminds us to think about all His benefits to us – God forgives, heals, redeems, loves, vindicates, and sustains.

In his book, *Sabbath: Remembering the Sacred Rhythm of Rest and Delight* (1999), Wayne Muller suggested that because we do not rest, we lose our way. The Sabbath is a day when we partake of the wisdom, peace and delight through play, refreshment and renewal. He suggested trying some of the following activities in addition to those mentioned above to help make the Sabbath what it should be.

- Light a candle during a family meal, or for meditation and prayer
- Practice thanksgiving throughout the day
- Bless your children and parents – let them hear your prayers for their peace and happiness
- Take a nap
- Prepare a special Sabbath meal – or a Sabbath cup of tea

- Spend time with a special friend, but don't talk business
- Create a Sabbath box – put your to-do list, wallet, car keys, and a list of your worries into the box. Just for now, let them go.
- Turn off the telephone, computer, and television. The outside world will be there when you return.
- Invite a Sabbath pause – choose a common act that is repeated several times throughout the day, like touching a door handle – when it occurs, pause and take several silent, mindful breaths

Soon this day will become something you look forward to all week. And maybe, just maybe, some of these actions will make their way into your other six days as well.

LUKE 13:18-21

The Growth of the Kingdom
(Matt. 13:31-33. Mark 4:30-32)

In this segment of Luke, Jesus presents us with two more examples of what God's kingdom is like. Both examples refer to the growth of the kingdom, but illustrate the contrast between inner growth and outer growth.

The well-known parable of the mustard seed dramatizes how one of the smallest of seeds can become a plant large enough to allow birds to build their nests in it. The kingdom of God was revealed to us by Jesus about two thousand years ago. This small seed has now grown to serve billions of people.

The kingdom of God is organized and serves under the banner of love, mercy and compassion, regardless of the denominational cover mankind puts on it. Jesus demonstrated numerous times that the kingdom of God cannot be packaged in the laws and methods of the Pharisees or scribes of his day, nor can it be corralled by the synods, dioceses, or parishes of ours. If it lives and breathes love, it's God's kingdom. The labels we tend to put on the kingdom tend to diminish its power, not enhance it.

The growth described above can be seen with the eye. It's like a plant growing in a garden plot. We know it gets bigger according to some divine plan, but we really don't know how this happens.

The other type of growth that Jesus mentioned is more subtle and unseen – at least at first. The kingdom of God is "like yeast that a woman took and mixed in with three measures of flour until all of it was leavened." The leaven is the inner growth of people within the kingdom. It consists of the ever-increasing consciousness about God and His love, and about the interconnectedness of all things in His kingdom.

As this awareness grows among the people, pieces of their false selves gradually drop off, like the scales from the eyes of Paul following his road to Damascus travels. They move toward enlightenment. They become more at peace, more understanding, and more powerful in a spiritual way. This change eventually manifests itself in greater service.

Inner growth fuels outer expansion. The outer expansion creates further room for inner growth. The two work together to gradually overcome the darkness of the world.

LUKE 13:22-30
The Gates of Heaven
(Matt. 7:13-14, 21-23)

Someone approached Jesus while he was making his way to Jerusalem, and asked him, "Lord, will only a few be saved?"

This question has been on people's minds through the ages. A traditional understanding is that at some point in time, the gates of heaven will be shut. Those that have "made it" will be safely inside, and those that didn't will be left outside where there will be "weeping and gnashing of teeth" for eternity. But how many got into the kingdom? How many didn't? "What are my odds that I'll make it?" we wonder. "What are the criteria, anyway?"

It's scary when we think about it, because a lot is at stake. This concept of God's kingdom can be used as an effective control tool, and has been used that way throughout the centuries. It's a powerful motivator to get people to behave themselves, much like Santa Claus "who knows when you've been bad or good – so be good for goodness sake!"

For many of us today, this uncertainty lurks in the far corners of our minds, occasionally disturbing our quieter moments. We wonder how a loving, compassionate God could do this to people. How could He punish someone for an eternity for the misdeeds of a few decades? Or even one mistake? Is this justice?

Our Western minds have evolved a concept of God's kingdom that is based on our own concept of justice. We interpret scripture and build our religious systems based on the idea that justice is served when we find the guilty people and punish them for their crimes. We want to "get even," and make the perpetrators pay in time and money. We justify our actions based on what we think is the "eye for an eye" in Judaic Law. We take these concepts and build an image of God around them. We create God in our own image.

God's concept of justice, however, is quite different. It's better defined from an Eastern approach to the resolution of issues, and has to do with restoration, healing, and making things whole again. An "eye for an eye" does not mean that if someone causes the blindness of another person, that the perpetrator is then blinded to make things even. It means that the perpetrator must now serve as the eyes of the one he blinded, making that victim whole again at some level.

Biblical justice always seeks to restore things to the way they were before the incident, *and* to determine why the incident occurred in the first place. There is just as much compassion and concern for the perpetrator of the crime as there is for the victim. Certainly, the victim must be restored to what they were or what they had before the incident, but it's also important to find out what led the perpetrator to commit the crime in the first place.

This is an opportunity to find flaws in a social system, educational system, political system, or environmental system, and fix them. It does *not* absolve responsibility of the perpetrator, who must certainly repent and work to help restore the victim where that's possible. But it adds further responsibility unto society to reflect on the nature of the incident and *all* its contributing factors. Justice is not so simple as to just identify the criminal and punish him or her for the crime. Justice demands an introspection of society as well, with subsequent adjustments made to improve things for everyone.

How does this apply to God's kingdom? God's justice is to find a way to allow every person to return home to His kingdom in this life or the next. He does not seek to punish, but to heal, to restore, to bring things and people back to wholeness. The only thing that stands in the way of this goal is human free will. If people don't let go of their false self, their dysfunctional egos, then God can't reach the true self within the soul – because the people themselves block Him out.

As recorded in this passage of Luke, when someone knocks on the door to get into the kingdom, the reply was not, "I'm sorry, the gates are closed forever! Go away!" The reply was, "I *do not know who you are* – go away!" In other words, if Jesus knew who the person was, the gates would be opened. Jesus can't and won't recognize the layers of illusion that cover the soul – arrogance, prejudice, power, greed, hatred – anything not of God and His kingdom.

These things simply wouldn't fit through the narrow door – they're too big! Simplicity slides through fine, but avarice is too wide. Gentleness and mercy easily pass by, but excessive pride is too large. Meekness is welcome, but inflated egos just won't fit. The narrow door doesn't refer to the limited number of people who can enter; it refers to the type of people that will be able to fit through. Those with less will have more, those with more will have less; "some are last who would be first, and some are first who thought they would be last."

The gates of the kingdom of God are *never* permanently closed. Jesus never said they would be. There is no limit to the number of people who may eventually enter. Jesus said, "People will come from east and west, from north and south, and will eat in the kingdom of God."

LUKE 13:31-35

The Great Decision
(Matt. 23:37-39)

During Advent, we are told of Christ's coming, and we wait with much anticipation. Then, at Christmas, we are told of the stories of his arrival, and receive him with great joy. During Epiphany his ministry and message are revealed to us, and we marvel at it. In Lent, we are asked to accept him and allow our lives to be transformed by his Presence.

So, how's that going for you? How's that going for the world? Well, there are signs that it's working quite well in many places. If we look closely, we can see the Spirit actively working through the souls of individuals and groups, spreading the love of God through words and deeds that really help others. There are many great support groups, and people working to unite mankind with nature. Much of the good that happens is not seen by all, but it's there. And I, for one, think that most of what's happening in the world is good.

But, of course, there's still much work to do. If God is so loving and compassionate, if He holds the key to a unified world of love, if He can truly wipe away every tear and turn every anguish into joy, why is this Lenten decision to follow Him so hard to make and keep?

Why is there still so much violence? Why is our country fractured by a paralyzed government and general loss of purpose? Why is our health care system curing people of illnesses and broken bones, while breaking them up with astronomical costs? Why do some people have seven bathrooms in their home while others have to pee on the street?

Jesus came with a message of love and unity, but he is warned, "Herod wants to kill you." Paul writes to the Philippians and says, "For many live as enemies of the cross of Christ ... Their end is destruction; their god is the belly; and their glory is in their shame; their minds are set on earthly things."

"Their minds are set on earthly things." Therein lies the core problem – free-will decisions that are heavily influenced by earthly things (i.e., mankind's delusions and essential survival instincts). Devoting your life to Christ can often be in direct opposition to your natural human tendencies of physical safety and survival.

Built into our instincts and brain wiring is the desire to live in safety and security, and as a result we often feel the need to get as much as we can, whatever it is, to satisfy that survival need. We are deeply afraid of not succeeding at this. Our marketing systems, economic systems, political systems, and social systems are designed to feed off of this fear, which pits people against people in a winner-take-all environment. This influence is very powerful and separates us into disconnected individuals. And this is where the delusion begins.

The odd thing, however, is that this need for survival and security is a God-given drive – He wants us to survive, to be safe, and to prosper, too. But in His case, He wants it used for the common good. That's where we, as humans, tend to slip up. The abundance of the world must raise us beyond the shallow waters of the human mind and lead us into the depths of spiritual love. We must rise above the fear of scarcity and embrace the faith in a system based on a united human family.

It all begins with the individual, you and me, making the Lenten decision to live a life based on the love of God in Christ. And although this decision begins with an individual choice, bringing it to fruition requires a solid network of support. Having like-minded people join you on this quest is the best way to overpower those forces that would prefer that you fail – the Herods of this world; the enemies of the soul.

Making this decision for Christ is only the first step. The rest is a journey we take with those who can support us. When we stumble, they help to pick us up. When they stumble we help them, too. Unity, love, and peace are the result.

LUKE 14:1-14

In the Presence of a Noble

In Luke 14, Jesus elaborated on Prov. 25:6-7, which reads, "Do not put yourself forward in the king's presence or stand in the place of the great; for it is better to be told, 'Come up here,' than to be put lower in the presence of a noble." For Jesus warned, "All who exalt themselves will be humbled, and those who humble themselves will be exalted."

Normally, I don't think I'm in danger of exalting myself, since I would rarely, if ever, be in the presence of a king, or a noble. But what about all the strangers in a store or on the street – could there be kings and nobles in our midst? How can we tell? Most of them aren't dressed in royal purple, but rather in humble attire. They aren't buying anything in particular that would suggest a higher status in society; not saying anything that would demonstrate an advanced education or worldly throne. They're not followed by an entourage to serve their slightest whim.

And yet, perhaps they've endured some hardship far greater than what I could have ever survived. Do I know whether they've cradled the head or held the hand of a dying loved one? What troubles have they endured with the kind of great patience and resiliency that I will never see? What losses have they suffered? With what loneliness have they been burdened? What have they experienced that I don't fully understand?

Aren't these people the true kings and nobles of this world? And who *wouldn't* be included in this royal cadre?

If they *all are* kings and nobles in God's eyes, then they all deserve the reverence and respect in each and every moment I encounter them; regardless of how they might have treated me, regardless of how they look, regardless of who they think they are, or regardless of who they really are.

Today you will walk among kings and nobles. Where will you seat yourself?

LUKE 14:15-24

There is Still Room
(Matt. 22:1-10)

The parable in this passage of Luke shows us that God's kingdom is open to anyone who accepts the invitation. It isn't an exclusive club for a select few, but instead is designed to welcome any and all of God's children. And yet, many still decline the offer.

The great dinner in the story is the divine nourishment offered in God's kingdom not only throughout eternity, but to us here and now as well. "The kingdom of God is near," Jesus taught us. It's available to us in this earthly life, beginning right now. The main entry gate to the kingdom is bringing our consciousness to the full awareness of God's love through the knowledge of our true selves, and how we are all children of God.

But our journey to the kingdom is sometimes waylaid by human instincts, physical survival needs, social pressures, and excessive competition which gradually grow scales over our hearts in the form of fear, arrogance, prejudice, hatred, and self-pride. We can no longer access the heart because the serpent ego has now wrapped itself around it. The gate to the kingdom has been blocked.

Attachments to possessions can be more attractive than being possessed by God. "I bought a piece of land, and I must go see it – please accept my apologies," said one man. Material goods are solid objects – they can be seen and felt and counted. They represent safety, success, and security. And it's understandable how this happens to us because of our physical vulnerabilities in this world. We gather material things to secure us in a material world. But, of course, it doesn't work in the long run because all physical objects change – they erode, rot, devalue, or get blown away – nothing will stay the same in this physical world, including our bodies.

Some people become *attracted to achievement*. They have no time for a banquet because "time is money." "I've bought five yoke of oxen, and I am going to try them out; please accept my apologies," the man said. He is stuck on the treadmill of production and is overdosing on competition. But this, too, is fueled by the fear of never having enough, and identifying with accomplishments and rewards rather than on one's own personal soul. The ego loves to compare itself to determine its worth. If it sees that it has more than someone else, it is happy for a moment – until it sees someone who has more. One pair of oxen is needed to feed his family; five pair are needed to feed his ego.

Other people fail to realize that God's kingdom has a place in their family. "I have just been married, and therefore I cannot come." Instead of bringing his partner to the banquet, he stays away. He failed to realize that relationships built on God's love are more solid than those built on material wealth.

But God is not deterred. He sends His messengers out ever further, seeking more and more people to come to the banquet until the hall is filled. It's not God who blocks people from entering the kingdom – people make the decision to stay away. Their treasure is elsewhere, and that's where they stay. But we must remember that the gate to the kingdom is not forever closed to those with a hard heart. At some point they may awaken to discover their true selves, and return home once again to the God who loves them.

LUKE 14:25-35

The Total Disciple
(Matt. 5:13; 10:37-38. Mark 9:50)

In Luke 14 Jesus presents a large crowd with a collage of somewhat challenging parables and conditions for those interested in following him. After hearing these, it wouldn't be surprising if the large crowd thinned out a little – maybe a lot.

Did Jesus really tell us to hate our father and mother, wife and children, brothers and sisters, and even life itself? Do we really have to carry the cross like he did? Does this mean we have to be crucified? Do we really have to fight in a battle? Are we going to fight armies when the odds are 2-to-1 against us? Must we give up all our possessions?

Jesus's words in Luke 14 may have been the inspiration of the all-familiar Christian hymn:

Onward, Christian soldiers, marching as to war,
with the cross of Jesus going on before.
Christ, the royal Master, leads against the foe;
forward into battle see his banners go!

Whoa! Whatever happened to "Come unto me all you who are weary and burdened, and I will give you rest?" (Matt. 11:28)

We're a war-weary nation. And our personal lives are filled with job struggles, family struggles, health issues, money problems, and a plethora of other worries. Who needs more trouble? The cost to be a disciple of Christ may be too high; the standards may be too demanding.

Maybe, just maybe, Jesus was talking about something else, and we need to rethink this passage. This section of Luke has occasionally been labeled "the Cost of Discipleship." Actually, the title should be something like, "The Way to Become Totally Human."

The main purpose for being a "Christian soldier" is to wage war against our own false self – all the illusions, prejudices, shame, hatred, anger, arrogance, anxiety, inferiority, superiority, false attachments and addictions that are the real enemies of life. For us to become who God made each of us to be, for us to serve Him in the place that we've been put in life, all these false things must die. We must bring harmony to our spiritual, emotional and psychological parts.

Jesus was giving us some guidelines to help us look inward, to help us straighten out our inner self, so that we can become truly human on the outside. And when this happens, we serve Him in all matters of life, large and small, in our own unique way, using the personal gifts and talents that He gave to each of us.

Jesus did not say to hate father and mother. (Good heavens! There's a commandment that says we should honor our father and mother!) The word *hate* is a mistranslation of the original Aramaic word which means "love less." Jesus was simply saying that it's important to keep things in perspective. A relationship with Jesus is the most important relationship we can have in this life. The love we have for him then becomes the basis of the relationship with have with anyone else: father, mother, wife, children, brothers, sisters, and even life itself. We soon begin to see the image of Jesus in other people, realizing that they, too, are children of God.

We must "carry the cross." What does this mean? The cross has become a symbol of Jesus's death and resurrection to a new life – that of Christ. We, too, must go through this – our old self must die so that our true self can live. It's not always easy, and can sometimes be painful. I know I'm still working on it. But we can't be truly human the way God wanted us to be, until we let some things go.

The tower parable and the warring kings parable remind us to proceed with caution and with the appropriate help. Becoming truly human is a journey best done as a team. We must take an honest, personal inventory, and then determine the best course of transformation.

But we can't do this alone. Many of us will do this with the help of counselors, therapists, physicians, psychologists, pastors, friends, and pets. We'll use the tools of prayer, meditation, journaling, talking, listening, walking, sleeping, and proper diets. It might take time – lots of time, but that's OK.

We will learn to seek peace with ourselves instead of waging war.

And don't forget to give up all your possessions! Really? And end up standing naked on the street corner? I don't think so.

Jesus knows that *attachment* to things greatly interferes with personal, spiritual growth. If the only way to get rid of the attachment to the thing is to get rid of the thing, then so be it. Again, he's trying to keep things in perspective. Material goods are to be used in an appropriate manner. But they are just things and will all eventually corrode, rot, wear out, get dusty, and fall apart (including our own bodies).

Not so with your soul. Not so with God. These things are eternal, and will continue to grow in God's love forever. We should use material things to help each other become fully human, to make sure as physical beings we all have sufficient food, clothing and shelter. But we also can share our creative output – our stories, pictures, gardens, sculptures, music, and ideas – things that also make us fully human.

The more we find our true selves, and the more we become who God made us to be, then the more we positively impact this world as a Christian soldier. We win huge battles for God when we can lend a helping hand to someone near us, in moment by moment personal interactions, as we go through our day. To glorify God is to become who He made us to be – unique, loving, interdependent people that reflect the love of God in each moment of life.

LUKE 15:1-10

Growing in God
(Matt. 18:12-14)

I grew up in a house that was only a few hundred feet from Highway 59, a busy Wisconsin road that connected Milwaukee with Waukesha. As I look back on those early years, I realize what a challenging job my mother had trying to keep watch over four young sons who constantly tested their boundaries (and her patience).

To help keep us safe, Mother had a rule about Highway 59: "Don't cross that road until you're 15 years old! Don't even go near it!" She said this with the authority of Moses coming down from Mt. Sinai carrying the Word of God, and backed it up with the fear of Grandma Hilma. If we boys got out of line, our mother would skip past the power of the county sheriff and the power of God, and call directly on Grandma.

I don't have many memories of Grandma Hilma, but I do remember that she was someone to fear. If we got too close to Highway 59 (or committed some other heinous offense), it would trigger an appearance by her at our front door that would startle the devil.

The four of us lads all made it into adulthood with few scars, and we kept all our fingers and toes, and we never did "poke our eyes out with that stick." The strict rules, and harsh consequences for violating them, were expertly administered out of love for us immature, but fast-growing boys.

There had to be rules, and there had to be a force behind them, or we might not have made it to puberty. The rules aptly fit the situation. It didn't always seem loving to us at the time, but it was indeed. As we grew older, the rules changed, and the expression of love changed with it. Eventually the rules faded away, and were replaced by adult expectations of mutual love and respect.

The story of God's love for mankind follows a similar pattern. Early on, in Old Testament times, strict rules were given to an emerging nation so that they, too, didn't cross the forbidden highway of life until they were mature enough. The patriarchs and prophets put the fear of God into the people's young hearts, something that they might best understand at that point in their journey to human wholeness.

Over time, hundreds of years actually, the fear of God was gradually replaced with a deeper understanding of His love for us – just as I eventually realized that the occasional harshness of my mother and grandmother was based on love. The tender, loving and sensitive moments far outnumbered the less comfortable times.

At the appropriate time in history, God Himself came to us in the person of Jesus. This loving God wanted to be with us to teach us, to heal us, and to demonstrate how love between us all should work. He came at a time when his words and life story could be recorded and shared with others, and passed down through all time. His earthly life and spiritual ascension also opened our hearts, even today, for His words about love continue through His advocate and teacher, the Holy Spirit.

The readings in Luke 15 actually give us some deeper insight into what His love is really like. The action taken by the shepherd defies economic and mathematical sense. Who would chase after one lost sheep while leaving the other 99? Doesn't it make more sense to cut your losses and stay with the 99?

Not so with God. The math of God is $1 = 99$. Or $1 = 1,000,000$ for that matter. Each and every person has an equal worth to Him. Any one person is important enough to Him that

He will continue to pursue that person to bring him or her back into the flock. No hesitation, no weighing the costs.

Even Paul, in writing to Timothy, states that he (Paul) received mercy because he had acted ignorantly in unbelief. He was a blasphemer, a persecutor of the early Christians, and a man of violence. But passing judgment is not as clear-cut as we may think it is in our world of justice today. God's love and mercy considers the context of a situation, not just the situation itself. His judgment considers the background of a person, the circumstances surrounding the behavior, and the extent of remorse. It's a far more complex decision than we usually care to deal with in our system of judgment.

Ps. 51 has sometimes been called the Psalm of Final Judgment. It might actually be a description of what we refer to as the Day of Judgment. The psalmist asks for mercy, according to God's steadfast love: "According to your abundant mercy blot out my transgressions." (v.51:1) He begs to be washed thoroughly, and cleansed from his sin.

On that day, the full realizations of his life become openly known to him – he realizes how both his good actions and his bad actions have impacted others in deep ways. He understands the joy and the pain that came from these. "You desire truth in the inward being; therefore teach me wisdom in my secret heart," he asks. "Create in me a clean heart, O God, and renew a right spirit within me."

Someday, perhaps, we will even look to the Day of Judgment as a good thing, as we grow in the understanding of God's love. We will come to realize that this Day will not be one of punishment and retribution, but one of renewal, reconciliation, and revival for every soul. It may actually be the beginning of a new life of love and service to God; one that goes on forever in a mutual understanding of what love is really all about.

The core of this love is best described by Paul in Rom. 8: "For I am convinced that neither death, nor life, nor angels, nor rulers, nor things present, nor things to come, nor powers, nor height, nor depth, nor anything else in all creation, will be able to separate us from the love of God in Christ Jesus our Lord."

LUKE 15:11b-32

Lost and Found – Two Prodigal Sons

This well-known story draws attention to a young son who squanders his inheritance in dissolute living. Having lost everything, and now in great need, he finds himself in a worse position than when he was back home, under his father's wing. The text goes on to say that eventually "he came to himself," which best means that he came to full realization of what he had done, and was now truly repentant.

Returning home, he planned to make a confession in hopes that he could salvage something of his previous place in the family. But as he approached his home, his father ran to him, and brushed aside the son's confession, being filled with joy that his son had returned to him. A celebration ensued, and the younger son was honored.

While we are glad that there was this family reunion, we may feel a bit cheated that this prodigal son, who wasted an inheritance, was honored instead of punished for his misdeeds. "Where is the justice in this?" we may ask. He was wasteful and reckless, and yet he was honored!

But if we look more closely, we see that the forgiveness of the father his huge merit. Did the son really go unpunished? First of all, he lost all his inheritance. This would impact his future for quite some time. Next, he was shamed into doing things that he wouldn't normally have done. He also feared that his family ties were destroyed; he was out of contact with his family, and didn't know if this relationship could be restored.

Finally, there was *the pain of awakening*. To finally come to the realization that others were harmed will cut deep into a soul. This is a burden that must be dealt with in some way, or it will never leave.

People who do things that hurt others are often suffering and in trouble themselves. They may have already been punished greatly in ways that we can't see. No, that doesn't give them the right to hurt others (and it doesn't mean that there should be no restitution, either), but it does provide a basis for understanding the entirety of the situation. Knowing what the other person went through might open the door for the possibility of forgiveness. The father of the prodigal son, like Our Father who made us, could see into the pain and suffering of each person, and is ready to receive anyone who truly wants to come back home. The young prodigal may have been disobedient, but he restored the heart connection to his father. This was most important to the father, just as it is to Our Father.

The second half of the story deals with the opposite situation, where the older son strictly obeyed his father's rules and wishes, but never was able to make the heart-to-heart connection. *Pure obedience without love is also a prodigal squandering, not of material wealth, but of spiritual riches.* The father was perhaps strongly hinting this idea to the older brother when he explained why they were celebrating the return of the younger son, "We had to celebrate and rejoice, because this brother of yours was dead (spiritually disconnected) and has come to life; he was lost and has been found."

Ps. 32 does well in summarizing the all-familiar story: "Happy are those whose transgression is forgiven, whose sin is covered. Happy are those to whom the Lord imputes no iniquity, and in whose spirit there is no deceit."

LUKE 16:1-13

On Serving God through Wealth

Jesus tells a story about a rich man and the rich man's money manager, who has been accused of mismanagement. Out of concern for his own future, the manager plans to make friends with those who owe money to the rich man, so he gives them a break on their debt. Why? If the manager loses his job, he may be able to count on some of those debtors for support.

The rich man is indeed a symbol of God – for who can be richer in what is valued most? And the money manager is, well, you and me and everyone else. We are managing some amount of God's riches, whoever we are, in the gifts of talent, abilities, and interests we have. They're really on loan from God.

We note from the reading that charges were brought against the money manager – it doesn't say that the charges were valid or proven; it just says that the money manager was being accused of mismanagement. And who is the complainant? Could it be that ol' Accuser himself, the devil? He would like to get everyone in trouble.

God, the rich man, is telling the manager that his time is up, and soon he can no longer be a manager. God is asking for an accounting of this person's business; his life. Perhaps the manager is being called home to God, and must now provide a record of how he lived.

The manager knows his time is running out, that his "position is being taken away." So, with the knowledge that his time is coming to an end, he realizes that he must do as much good as he can before the end comes. Under his authority as money manager, he goes out and begins to forgive the debtors of some of their debt. It's an act of kindness that not only relieves the debtors of some of their monetary burden, but also, he hopes, paves the way for God to forgive him.

The rich man, when he learned of this act, wasn't mad that he wouldn't be collecting all that was owed to him, but instead commended the accused manager for his shrewdness. (Some translations read "dishonest manager," but we must remember that he wasn't convicted, only accused.) The rich man was pleased that forgiveness was happening; he considered forgiveness to be more valuable than collecting his due.

Jesus reinforced the story by adding, "Make friends of those oppressed by unfair financial burdens, so that when this life is over, they may be able to help you in the next." His point was that the rich can help the poor in this age, and then the poor can help the rich in the age to come.

Jesus went on to explain that the action of the money manager wasn't done out of the fear of God, but out of the love for God's creation and all His children. He warns us that we cannot serve both the love of God and the love of money – these are incompatible. We will "either hate the one and love the other, or be devoted to the one and despise the other."

Jesus often spoke out against financial oppression; the use of power and influence to gain more wealth by oppressing others. Amos reinforces this idea very well: "Hear this, you that trample on the needy, bringing to ruin the poor of the land, and say 'we will overcharge for the sale, and practice deceit with false balances, buying the poor for silver and the needy for a pair of sandals...' Surely, says the Lord, I will never forget any of their deeds." (Amos 8)

Remember, however, wealth is not the problem. It can be a good thing if acquired properly, and used wisely. Wealth can be the impetus for positive change in this world, and often is. But it can also be abused just as easily. It all depends on where your heart is, because that's where your treasure is, too.

Paul sums this idea up well in his letter to Timothy when he writes, "God our Savior desires everyone to awaken to His truth." (v. 2:4) It is truth of love and wholeness, not of threat or retribution. It is a truth of healing and unity, not of division and spite.

LUKE 16:14-18

Thy Kingdom Come
(Matt. 5:31-32; 11:12-13. Mark 10:11-12)

Jesus proclaimed a turning point in history when he said, "The law and the prophets were in effect until John came; since then the good news of the kingdom of God is proclaimed."

And what was this good news that was now being proclaimed? It's the truth about God's love for all His creation and His children. It's an unconditional love that is available for everyone who will receive it. It's a love, Paul points out, that is unstoppable by anything in the entire universe, with the exception of our ability to reject it.

The kingdom of God offers the wisdom we need to live in today's world, bringing to it a depth of peace, collaboration, kindness, abundance, joy, and patience. It's the outpouring of the gifts of the Holy Spirit unto the world and its people. (Gal. 5:22-23)

God's kingdom can only be accessed by those who are ready to receive it. But those people who are ruled by their dysfunctional egos (false selves) are not able to see the kingdom; they don't understand the benefits of it, nor do they believe anything like that could work in the world. They prefer to rely on the system that mankind has developed over the centuries, a system based on money that has plenty of surface attractions, but which creates great social and economic inequities, material waste, and long-term environmental damage.

"What is prized by human beings is an abomination in the sight of God," explains Jesus. He's speaking generally about the love of money. When it replaces the love for God and His wisdom, people get hurt, God's creatures suffer, and the world as a whole suffers. The good news of God is the key to world healing and fulfillment. "Thy kingdom come, Thy will be done, on earth as it is in heaven."

Access to the kingdom and all its benefits can only be reached through our true selves. This is the original soul-self that was given to us by God, and contains within it the ability to tap into the resources and wisdom of the kingdom. It's easy for the soul-self to access the kingdom of God because the soul-self is a direct product of the kingdom. It comes to us with ready-made connections that are free and open and easy to use.

People eventually come to realize that the kingdom of God is the answer not only for themselves, but also for the world. They awaken to the fact that they have been living an illusion, and have not, in reality, been living their true lives. When they reach this point, they may attempt to fight their ego directly, using various self-disciplinary methods, asceticism, or self-abasement. Direct assault upon the ego only makes it stronger (aggression breeds resistance). This is what Jesus meant by his statement regarding the kingdom, that "everyone tries to enter it by force."

But you can't force your way into the kingdom. Why? Because you're already in it! Jesus said that you are the temple of God. How can you force your way into something that you're already in? You just have to realize that you're in it.

Awareness of your false self is the first, and most powerful, weapon to dislodging it. By simply awakening to its presence and what it is doing to your thought processes is 80 percent of the battle. Do not resist it; but accept it without judgment, and acknowledge it for what it is and for what it may have done to you. It begins to shrink away in the Light of Truth.

Now begin to fill in the gaps with further knowledge and practice about God's love. This is what the law and the prophets were designed to do, and why Jesus said they will not be dropped. Study them! This is your monastic practice. Become who God made you to be, and then reach out into your own world and use the unique skills, talents, and interests you have in whatever way that helps someone else and the world around you.

LUKE 16:19-31
Lazarus and the Rich Man

Economic disparity has plagued mankind since the rise of civilization. The parable in Luke 16 presents one such example, and is thought to be based on a story that went back even further in time. One person in the story has way too much wealth – more than he'll ever need, "feasting sumptuously every day." Another person in the story lays homeless at the rich man's doorstep, suffering from lack of food. Even in the United States today, one of the richest countries in the world, there are millions of homeless people while some people don't even know how many homes they have! Thousands of people in the world die each year from starvation, while others die from diseases caused by eating too much food.

But it wasn't always this way.

Anthropologists report that before the rise of complex economic systems, small bands or tribes of people worked together and shared their resources. Everyone had an opportunity to help in a way that they could, and each received a portion of the hunt or the harvest. With the rise of innovation and the complexity of trade, a medium of exchange developed (money) that assigned values to labor and material goods. The use of money brought with it the opportunity for profit and the accumulation of wealth. And when this occurred, some people began to have more, and others began to have less. It was fodder for the development of dysfunctional egos based on power, superiority, greed, and fear of scarcity.

The main underlying causes of economic disparity (and the subsequent growth of dysfunctional egos) are fear and isolation. Fear, because we think that we won't have enough to survive here on Earth. And isolation, because we believe that there really isn't anyone out there who will help us if we get into trouble, because they, too, are scrambling to get enough – and, of course, enough is never enough. The ego always wants more.

The rich man in this parable, "dressed in purple and fine linen," has succeeded in this economic system, and he's not about to lose any of it. Therefore his ego has encapsulated his soul, and he can no longer see the needs of others around him. He's built a chasm around him that becomes impenetrable from any direction.

He steps over the withering bodies of those people at his gate who couldn't cope in a world of stiff competition. He might even drop a few crumbs from his bountiful table to ease his withering conscience, doing just enough to offer the appearance of being compassionate. But the economic disparity still exists, and while it destroys the body of the poor, it destroys the soul of the greedy rich.

Eventually, however, mortality catches us all, and the parable reports that both men eventually pass over to the next life. We find Lazarus enjoying the kingdom to its fullest. The rich man, however, *has brought his chasm with him*. He still thinks that he's better than Lazarus as seen by his suggestion to Abraham that Abraham send Lazarus to serve him! He just doesn't get it. Until the rich man awakens to the presence of his dysfunctional ego, he remains trapped in it. No one can reach him, nor can he connect with anyone else. He won't be able to make the final transition into the kingdom as long as he remains blinded by his own ego. Jesus pointed out that even someone returning from the dead to warn him would probably not convince him.

Some people will gradually awaken to their true self (and the ego that has surrounded it) through continuous exposure to the truth – the Light – that comes from God. Some people reach the point of enlightenment only after losing everything in some disaster. They go from riches to rags quickly, and realize that there has to be more to life than the attachment to things and money. Other people may never change, even after passing from this life to the next, like the rich man in the parable.

As we've so often heard, it isn't money that's the problem – it's the *love* of money that's the root of evil. And that love of money comes from the illusion that having a limitless supply of it will save us from the perils of life. But, of course, it doesn't – it's only an illusion. Yes, we all need some money for basic living needs, but there comes a point when too much is just too much.

Dismantling the current economic structure will not solve the problems of fear and isolation that feed egos. The key is the awakening of people to their true selves; to the fact that while they are physical beings with real physical needs, they are also part of a world-wide family of God. They need to learn that the earth has abundant resources to share, and no one has to suffer for the lack of them. It's everyone's responsibility to ensure economic equity in whatever way they their life permits.

LUKE 17:1-10

She Did What She Could
(Matt. 18:6, 7, 21, 22. Mark 9:42)

At one point when Jesus had been teaching his disciples, they requested, "Increase our faith!" It appears that this request pleased Jesus, because he affirmed how powerful faith could be: "If you had faith the size of a mustard seed, you could say to this mulberry tree, 'Be uprooted and planted in the sea,' and it would obey you."

But what, exactly, is faith? Some people would say that faith is essentially belief; others might say that faith is when the soul has trust in the unseen future – when belief and confidence far outweigh the fear and uncertainty of the mind. Faith comes with a growth in spiritual maturity.

What follows in this Gospel text must then be viewed with an eye toward spiritual growth. If God indeed is love, then this spiritual growth would therefore be based in love, and nothing else. So, understanding the passage in Luke 17, like all scriptural understanding, must be viewed from a loving standpoint.

Jesus continues with an example of what this love would look like between a master and his servant, "Who among you would say to your servant who has just come in from plowing or tending sheep in the field, 'Come here at once and take your place at the table?'" Jesus crosses the barriers of social and economic class, putting *everyone* at his table.

Then he describes what we (generally speaking) would normally do based on social norms: "Would you not rather say to him, 'Prepare supper for me, put on your apron and serve me while I eat and drink; later you may eat and drink'?" We may prefer to maintain the divide in social and economic class – but Jesus would prefer that we treat each person as an equal, as a brother or sister in the Lord.

Next, in verse 9, comes an admonishment: "Do you thank the servant for doing what was commanded? I think you don't." But, of course, you should, is the implication.

But this class abuse doesn't stop when dealing with other people. We also do this to ourselves, as well: "So you also, when you have done all that you were ordered to do, say, 'We are worthless servants; we have done only what we ought to have done!'"

To grow spiritually, to increase our faith, we must put ourselves in the proper frame of mind. Jesus does not want to add burdens to us, making us think that no matter what we do with our lives, it's never enough. This is a guilt trip that burdens our soul, interferes with our love, and inhibits spiritual understanding.

Remember what Jesus said about burdens: "Come to me, all you that are weary and are carrying heavy burdens, and I will give you rest. Take my yoke upon you, and learn from me; for I am gentle and humble in heart, and you will find rest for your souls. For my yoke is easy, and my burden is light." (Matt. 11:28-30)

And remember when the woman came to him at Bethany with an alabaster jar of very costly ointment? She used it to anoint Jesus, but was criticized because she did not meet the expectations of those around her. Jesus rebuked them, saying, "She has done what she could." (Mark 14: 3-9)

It is not Jesus's intent to have us burn out in life and still feel like we fall short of salvation. Our lives will be full indeed, and we will serve others best when we fill our hearts with love. We need balance in our lives to function properly – rest, solitude, study, prayer, and nourishment must balance out our mission and service, or we'll self-destruct. We must let Jesus decide that we've "done what we could," and not base our lives on the standards of society, peers or our own inner illusions.

Faith is knowing that the present moment is the womb of the future. If we fill each and every moment with our best effort at God's love, then the future will indeed be the best that it can be. Once again we can leave the past to God's mercy, and the future to His Providence.

LUKE 17:11-19

The Four Degrees of Love

About a thousand years ago, St. Bernard, Abbot of Clairvaux, wrote about what he called the four degrees of love. These degrees of love suggest a gradual development of love within a person, much like the physical or intellectual development of a person from birth through old age.

Most people begin life just trying to survive. Some people struggle for the basics of food, clothing, shelter, and security most of their lives, through no fault of their own. They develop a survival mentality that carries over into their relationships which never has the chance to grow into something more beautiful. People in this first degree of love, according to St. Bernard, usually *love themselves for their own sake.*

Perhaps the nine lepers who didn't return to give thanks to God were at this basic level of love. They were healed, and possibly attributed this healing to their good fortune, without the slightest thought of gratitude to God or anyone else.

A slightly more spiritually mature approach was the one taken by the lone leper who returned to Jesus to praise God "with a loud voice." This reflects what St. Bernard would call the second degree of love, where *a person loves God, but still for his or her own sake.* The person realizes where his or her help originated, and as the psalmist declares, "I lift up my eyes to the hills; from where will my help come? My help comes from the Lord, who made heaven and earth." (Ps. 121:1-2) God is loved as a provider of help and comfort.

If this happens enough, St. Bernard suggests, then the person may actually begin to understand the nature of God's love, exclaiming as did the psalmist, "O taste and see that the

Lord is Good..." (Ps. 34:8) At this point the person actually begins to *love God for God's sake*. This is the third degree of love. As in loving other people for their sake, we wish the best for them, we try to help them, we promote them because of who they are, not because of who we are, and sometimes it may even cost us something to do so.

Paul reaches (and often goes beyond) this point. We see an example of this third degree of love when he writes to Timothy, "I endure everything for the sake of the elect..." He is willing to endure hardships to promote his belief in Christ, "even to the point of being chained like a criminal." He loves because he is loved. (2 Tim. 2:9, 10)

At some point, says St. Bernard, a person may reach the fourth degree of love. It may not happen in this lifetime, but eventually the person will be made complete in this love, either in this life or the next. And what is this state of love? It's when things come full circle, and people learn to *love themselves for the sake of God*! It's at that point that people understand that they are actually temples of God, that God abides within them, and they abide in God.

As Jesus taught us, "the kingdom of God is within you." We pray daily through the words of the Lord's Prayer: "Thy kingdom come, Thy will be done, on earth as it is in heaven." This is accomplished by us becoming like God, and living as though God were working through us. Saint Teresa of Avila said it well when she wrote the prayer, "Christ has no body now on earth but yours, no hands but yours, no feet but yours. Yours are the eyes through which Christ's compassion is to look out to the world. Yours are the feet with which Christ is to go about doing good."

This is the fourth degree of love. Realizing that we are all one family, all brothers and sisters, under One God, our Parent.

We learn, because of this interconnectedness, that what affects one of us, affects all of us to some degree. As St. Paul writes in I Cor. 12, "If one member suffers, all suffer together with it; if one member is honored, all rejoice together with it."

Ten lepers were healed, but only one of them was on the path to being made "well." Jesus recognized the difference between being healed (physically), and being well (spiritually). The one leper was now on the path through the degrees of love, on the path to being human, on the path to becoming whole, to becoming an instrument of God here on Earth.

LUKE 17:20-37

Serving the Kingdom
(Matt. 24:23-28, 37-41)

A good friend and spiritual brother of mine wrote to me about his deep-felt sorrow and frustration over the state of the world: extremists using foreign weapons to commit atrocities against other people in the Mideast; kidnapping of young girls from schools in Africa; Israel and Palestine carrying out their age-old grievances with guns, rockets and bombs; immigrant children fleeing oppression in Central and South America, and ongoing conflicts between races that spill over into violence.

These are just some of the bigger troubles. Many incidents of violence on the streets of every city in the world get buried beneath the news of larger conflicts. There is street crime, but also numerous cases of unreported abuse that leave lifelong emotional and physical scars on children.

So, what can I tell this friend? Certainly, the troubles of the world are there and must be acknowledged. Ignoring them won't make them go away. And, yes, we can counterbalance these dark reports with those on the brighter side: People *are* helping people and goodness is in abundance. It seems that as the evil grows, so does the goodness, but to a greater degree.

Still, we wonder and struggle over how to confront the bad that is happening. So much of it seems way beyond our power – and it is. But we don't like to feel helpless; we must believe that even some small thing we do will somehow contribute toward peace and harmony. We don't want to be powerless against these dark forces. We need to know that God is fully aware of what's happening in the world, and that somehow He'll make everything right, sooner or later.

History has repeatedly shown that when people turn their backs on the kingdom of God and its inherent wisdom, things tend to fall apart rather quickly. People lose their bearings and begin to rely on the systems that mankind has built to grow economies and the strength of nations. This, in turn, gives rise to individual and collective dysfunctional egos that are willing to sacrifice a few people for the good of those who know the system and can manipulate it for their own good. Sometimes this evil is rooted in misguided, human-generated religious principles that nurture a merciless fanaticism. In its worst manifestation, it seeks ethnic cleansing that ends in brutal cases of genocide.

The kingdom of God is our only hope. But it's not a kingdom of castles and knights in shining armor on horses that come to slay the dragon of evil. It's not some distant army that we wait for to come and straighten out the world. "God's kingdom isn't something you can see," replied Jesus when the

Pharisees asked him when the kingdom would come. "God's kingdom is here within you."

God's kingdom works from the inside out, not from the outside in. It's an invisible kingdom that manifests itself in physical, seeable changes of good. The kingdom is within each person, but only accessible when the person decides to access it. It's recognizing the true inner self, the soul space, which was put there by God Himself. The true self reveals a person's true identity as a child of God – and opens the portal of the kingdom, allowing God's love to flow through to the outside world.

Getting people to recognize this, of course, is the major problem. So many people are asleep under the illusions offered by this physical world that they can't see beyond the surface. Some people gradually awaken to the truth, others never do. And when those in the deepest sleep ban together into a collective dysfunctional ego, terrible things can happen.

At some point, as we read in the rest of this selection from Luke, Jesus himself will return to take over the earth and set things up right. But the kingdom starts *now*, and will be fulfilled upon his return, so let's do what we can. We find out who we were made to be, and we do it.

We must always remember that what we do helps, however little we think it is. So keep doing it – *praying* to ground ourselves in the wisdom and love of God, *studying* to grow in knowledge and understanding of ourselves and the world, and *serving* to further His kingdom on Earth.

LUKE 18:1-8
Persistence and Prayer

Luke 18 provides a difficult passage that offers richness in possibilities. Commonly considered a lesson that persistent prayer brings results, we find that the reason for this perception is perhaps different from what we think. Let's remember that the widow in the story wasn't *praying* to the judge persistently, she was assertively confronting him until she won her case. But she probably couldn't have persevered unless she had the spiritual power to do so.

Jesus opens his lesson with two important points: the need to pray always, *and* not to lose heart. There was a widow, Jesus said, who sought justice from an unjust judge. This widow probably had no power or money, two things that are very advantageous in a worldly system of politics, greed and power. But the widow did have persistence! She finally got what she wanted by pestering the judge, never giving up.

She didn't give up pursuing her cause, which was one of Jesus's points to this story: Don't give up, particularly when battling a secular system that is indifferent to justice for all. Keep fighting for what is right and just, even when the odds seem insurmountable.

But how do we maintain the energy, the passion and the motivation to keep fighting the good fight? That is the second point Jesus was making: the need to pray always. The basic function of prayer is to get in touch with God, which ultimately gets us in touch with other people. When we do connect with God, we connect with His power source, His love for us and the world, and we are re-energized, refreshed, and renewed once again.

This is the balance we need in the dance of life – sometimes we need silent time, prayer time, contemplative time, and sometimes we are out engaging the world, serving as God's hands, feet, and voice in our day-to-day activities.

Jesus affirms that the unjust judge is unlike God by comparing how the judge responded to the woman with how *God* responds to His children: "Will He delay long in helping them [like the unjust judge]? I tell you, He will quickly grant justice to them." No need to beg, grovel or pester.

Justice in Biblical times had a broader meaning than what we think it is today. Back then, it meant to restore equity to a person – not just in monetary terms, but in a sense of wholeness as a human being. People became *just* when they were connected with God through prayer and were given the wisdom and understanding of His love. They achieved a harmony between mind, body and soul. Armed with this harmony, they could engage the world in a powerful way, to overcome even the worst of the unjust judges.

It's true that we need to be persistent in prayer, so that we have the energy to venture out and confront the wrongs in this world. The widow had the power to maintain her persistence because she prayed often.

Jesus concludes this lesson with an admonition: "When the Son of Man comes, will he find faith on Earth?" The person who stays secluded from the world will have little impact on it. But the person who never prays, who never takes time to renew, refresh, or recharge one's spiritual batteries will burn out too quickly, and also have little or no impact on the world. Once again, *balance* is the key.

LUKE 18:9-14
Mistaken Identity

One of the most important things that each of us must do in life is to find our true identity. We must know our roots, who we belong to, and what unique gifts, interests, and talents we have been given to become who we were made to be. This is a job of the heart, not of the head. If we let the head lead us, we could very well end up with a false identity.

"The secret of our identity lies in how we can reveal our inner quality of aliveness. When we fail to be who we really are, we sicken."
                              -Cynthia Bourgeault

Our true identity rests deep within our soul, waiting to be discovered, anxious to be released. Often, as we travel through life, our true identity gets covered up, like a dirty light bulb, with illusions, desires, prejudices, fears, arrogance, shame, or worry. We develop a false self, someone truly foreign to us, but who settles into mankind's system of things. The true self shining on the inside never makes it to the surface.

This was true of Saul until he encountered Jesus on the road to Damascus. Saul was a persecutor of the Church, sending some people to prison. On his way to Damascus to continue this persecution, he was intercepted by Jesus: "Saul, Saul, why do you persecute me?" (Acts 9:4) The encounter with Jesus caused temporary blindness in Saul, but eventually was relieved by Ananias, a disciple of the church.

Ananias laid hands on Saul, and "Immediately something like scales fell from Saul's eyes, and his sight was restored." The false self of Saul dissolved, and Saul's true self was able to shine through. From then on Saul (soon to be known as Paul) understood what the love of God was really about, and worked for the Church the rest of his life.

"To become God-like is to identify ourselves with the divine element which in fact constitutes our essential nature, but of which, in our mainly voluntary ignorance, we choose to remain unaware."
- Aldous Huxley

Jesus further described this huge difference between the false self and the true self in the parable recorded in Luke 18. Two men went to pray in the temple. The Pharisee was living through his false self, much like Saul was. He thought he was in God's good favor because he went above and beyond what the rules required. He thought the way to God was through his status and behavior. He was depending entirely on himself, a mistaken identity.

The other man, a tax collector, was at a different inner place. He had discovered his true self, and because of this he understood his connection with God and with other people, and how his thoughts, words, and deeds either hurt or helped God's creation. He grasped the idea that we're all interconnected, and connected with God. This discovery led him to changing his life, much as Saul did. In the words of Jesus, he will become "justified" – to be made complete as an individual that is part of the whole, a part of the family of God.

Some people discover their true identity early in life. Some people never do. It all depends on the thickness of the false self that covers the true self. A soft word or gentle touch might crack the tough exterior coating, or it might take a life-threatening situation or financial disaster. It Saul's case, it took an intervention by Christ himself.

Once we discover this inner true self, it gradually manifests itself in our outer purpose in life. We begin to make changes in our life that represent who and what we really are. Our outer life is in harmony with our inner identity. Some of these changes are risky, and may be costly in terms of material position and security, but they nevertheless lead us to a fullness in life that can't be achieved any other way. Our mind, body, and soul grow together in harmony.

One thing we must remember is that regardless of who we meet and deal with during the day, how irritable or annoying they may be, underneath what we see and hear rests a true self waiting to be discovered. Their false self is not all their fault – we don't know what they've been through in life, or what they're facing at the moment. So be gentle.

LUKE 18:15-17

The Fountain of Youth
(Matt. 19:13-15. Mark 10:13-16)

What we are born with as children is often what we need as adults to reclaim our soul. Children in their first few years of life seem to be connected to reality – that is, life as it should be. They are much better at this than adults. They seem to see things we can't, they notice things we've forgotten about, they enjoy the smallest discoveries, and they are honest about who they are. They seek and ask, they are truthful, they share, and they realize they need to connect with other people on a heart-to-heart basis to become whole.

When we carefully observe a child, we are reminded of what we've somehow lost as we struggle with life and with the fear of failing. We learn that honesty can be dangerous, especially around people who have power over us (or rather, to whom we have given that power). We project public images of ourselves that we think others will acknowledge and accept better than who we really are. We adopt illusory goals in life that we think will give us happiness, status, and security. We prostitute our time and talent, sometimes compromising deeper values we wish we could live by instead.

Although a lost path through life might be called "sinful" by some, it's actually something to be healed, not punished.

So at some point in life, we begin to become aware of the cost of cheating our true selves, and we begin to make the journey back home. It's an Exodus, an escape from bondage, so that we can begin the journey back to wholeness. We gradually figure out ways to reclaim our soul by seeking to reconnect with our true inner self and with other people of like mind.

Jesus knew that children are the key to the kingdom. So did some parents, and that's why they brought their children to Jesus to be blessed. Cultural norms, however, kept children from "bothering" adult happenings. The disciples told the parents to stop bothering Jesus. But Jesus called the children over to him and said, "Let the children come to me! Don't try to stop them. People who are like these children belong to God's kingdom. You will never get into God's kingdom unless you enter it like a child!"

Children have much to learn about life as they grow up and find their way in society. But adults have much to learn from children, too. They are reminders of what we might have lost along the way, keeping us from connecting with reality – the truth about who we really are and why we're here on this planet.

The kingdom of God is within you, said Jesus. It's already here with us. But to realize its potential and its benefits, we must be able to receive it. We need certain qualities found in the mind of a child to lift the gate that separates us from the kingdom: trust, curiosity, sharing, awareness, mindfulness, patience, compassion, joy, gratitude, humility, interdependence and simplicity. Perhaps we'll begin to see things we have never seen before – at least not since we were little children. We might even begin to look at our social systems and educational systems to change what may be robbing the children of these gifts as they grow older.

The journey back to the kingdom is an open invitation by our Creator. It's not always easy, and progress may be slow, but there is no other true path for us. Once you're on it, you won't want to turn back.

LUKE 18:18-30

Thy Kingdom Come, Thy Will Be Done
(Matt. 19:16-30. Mark 10:17-31)

One of the ideas in Biblical times about wealth (and perhaps still believed by some people today) was that prosperity was a blessing to righteous people and a sign of God's favor. Jesus, however, would have none of this, and used the incident of the wealthy man in this segment of Luke to teach about it.

The story tells us about a wealthy man who ran up to Jesus, knelt before him, and asked Jesus, "Good teacher, what must I do to inherit eternal life?" Perhaps he thought Jesus would praise him for all the good things the man had done.

Jesus responded to the question by first reminding the man that it was only proper to consider God alone as being good, since God was the source of all goodness. "Why do you call me good? No one is good but God alone." Every devout Jew felt this way about God.

Jesus continued, "You know the commandments," and then listed a few of them that specifically had to do with interpersonal relationships: Do not murder, do not steal, honor your father and mother. The man responded to Jesus, "Teacher (now dropping off the 'good' part), I have kept all these since my youth."

Jesus had the sensitivity to look past a person's crusty outer ego into the heart, the part that he loved best in each person. Seeing a person's truest needs, Jesus was able to prescribe exactly what that person needed to move ahead in life. He saw that the wealthy man was attached to his wealth. This attachment was keeping him back. It was not the man's wealth that was the problem, but the problem was that the man's wealth had become his god. The man may have felt that he was given wealth because of his ability to keep all the commandments. He had over-inflated his importance and ability.

For this man, Jesus had a prescription: "You lack one thing," he pointed out, "Go, sell what you own, and give the money to the poor, and you will have treasure in heaven. Then, come, and follow me." This is what Jesus meant earlier when he said that if our hand offends us, cut it off and throw it away. The man's wealth had to be cut off in order for him to find God's kingdom.

But the wealthy man's attachment was too great. He was shocked at Jesus's suggestion, and went away grieved. He wasn't willing to trade his many possessions for a place in God's kingdom.

What was the wealthy man's fatal flaw? Perhaps it rested within his question to Jesus, "What must I *do* to inherit eternal life?" The man thought that accessing the kingdom of God could be done through deeds and effort. After all, he had followed every commandment since his youth, hadn't he? And yet, that wasn't good enough for Jesus.

Certainly, Jesus was a person of action. He thought action was important. But the *reasons* for doing the action were even more important. The wealthy man followed the commandments perfectly to gain access to the kingdom of God. But Jesus was trying to teach him that proper actions are done as a result of one's joy, love and devotion to God, not simply to gain something for ourselves. True action comes from the heart, not the head. Perfectly following all the laws misses the mark.

We can't win the kingdom of God for ourselves. The kingdom of heaven is a gift from God when we are ready for it, whether in this life or the next. It's given freely to those who would properly receive it. In Luke 12:32 we read, "Fear not, little flock, for it is your Father's good pleasure to give you the kingdom."

Fulfilling all of God's laws perfectly does not make you ready for the kingdom of God. The way to the kingdom is to remove all the things like prejudices, illusions, biases, sense of inferiority, hatred, worry, fear and shame so that the inner soul can shine forth. We work to become who God made each one of us to be, in our own uniqueness, joyfully serving Him in whatever life situation we find ourselves. We use our unique talents, gifts, and interests, along with the fruits of the Holy Spirit to reach our full potential.

The real question is, "What must I *be* to inherit eternal life?" The rest will follow according to His will. Then, the kingdom will be near to us. Remember this when you pray the Our Father: "Thy kingdom come, Thy will be done, on Earth as it is in heaven."

LUKE 18:31-34

It Was Bound to Happen
(Matt. 20:17-19. Mark 10:32-34)

Several times during his ministry Jesus predicted that he would eventually be arrested, mistreated, and killed. This was news that could not get past the mental filters of the apostles. They had a different idea of what was to come, an idea based on the early scriptures, traditions, and hopes of a people looking for a deliverer from their earthy oppression. The fact that Jesus, their mentor and guide, would be arrested and killed just didn't fit into their belief. So, they ignored this prediction, tried to interpret it in different ways, or directly attacked it as Peter did.

Jesus's eventual arrest and execution was a very dark moment in human history. Maybe the darkest. Knowing what we now know about that period in history, it's not surprising that certain people in power wanted him out of their way. It's also not too surprising that the differences in philosophies between Jesus and those in power would be great enough that it would result in Jesus's murder.

The message he was bringing to the people would disrupt the current power structure. Where he taught equity, others promoted a system where some had more wealth and material goods than others. Where he taught equality, others preferred a system where some enjoyed a higher status of privilege, while others were still considered to be inferior or just property to be bought, sold or traded. Where Jesus taught love, compassion and mercy, others built a system of punishment and retribution that was often used to control and manipulate. Jesus taught us how to dismantle collective ego structures, and how to find our true selves. But this would cause a power shift back to the people – a direct threat to those in authority at the time.

Early on in his ministry, Jesus went unnoticed. But when the crowds around him grew, and the people got excited about this new message, the leaders began to worry about their status. When they assessed that their losses would be too high, they plotted to remove Jesus.

Egos, especially collective egos, can go to extreme lengths to survive. Sometimes the dysfunctional ego ends up killing its host; other times it ends up killing the threat – in this case, Jesus. Mankind at its lowest point, completely separate from the wisdom and love of God, could even kill the Son of Man.

And there on the cross, the wounded Christ reflects the broken condition of mankind's soul at its lowest and most imprisoned state. It's what all the sins of the world look like; past, present and future. It's a mirror that shows us what we become when we trade our true selves for all the illusions of the world. It's through this broken image that we can see our dark selves clearly; we see the extent of what we are capable of doing to each other when we sink so low, rejecting the wisdom and guidance of God's love. It's through this broken image that we'll hopefully be shocked into realizing how far we have fallen, and thereby awaken to the truth of God's Light and Love. If it catches our heart and transforms us, we begin the path of salvation – the saving Grace of God – shedding our false selves and finding our true selves so that we can serve God in our own unique way, the way in which He made us.

Did Jesus preach the truth? Was he the Son of God? Does God really so love the world? How can we know this whole amazing story is real? What should convince us that Jesus was indeed the Son of Man? Perhaps the only way was for God to bring Jesus back to life, to defy even death, affirming to us God's approval and in effect saying, "Yes! This is my Beloved Son in whom I am well pleased! Listen to him!" Thus the significance and importance of the Resurrection.

The wisdom of Jesus, the cross on Calvary, and the resurrection are the core of the Gospel and the foundation of the Christian movement.

LUKE 18:35-43

Let Me See Again
(Matt. 20:29-34. Mark 10:46-52)

The meeting of Jesus and Bartimaeus appears to be a healing of Bartimaeus' sight, but may actually have been a healing of *insight*. In either case, there are things we can learn from this encounter.

Bartimaeus was a blind beggar sitting by the roadside just outside of Jericho. (We learn his name from the Gospel of Mark.) Jesus would be coming through there on his way to Jerusalem. Bartimaeus must have been aware of who Jesus was, and what power Jesus had. The scripture tells us that as soon as Bartimaeus heard that it was Jesus coming down the road, he shouted out, "Jesus, Son of David, have mercy on me!"

But what did this beggar want from Jesus? Especially right then, when Jesus was making his final journey to Jerusalem, where he would live his last days on Earth. The impertinence of this man to interrupt Jesus at this time caused others to intervene: "Don't bother Jesus," they said, "you are just a blind beggar. Jesus has no time for you." The people around Jesus sternly ordered Bartimaeus to be quiet. These voices came from the people around Jesus himself! How could this be? Weren't they followers of Jesus, disciples of his love?

Sometimes we encounter these same voices, too – people trying to block our way to Jesus. And sometimes these voices come from right inside our own head! We may be oppressed by what others try to tell us, or by our own sense of inferiority – "I am not worthy enough to be helped by God." Even though blind and poor, Bartimaeus knew he was still a child of God, no greater, nor lesser, a person than anyone else in the eyes of God. Bartimaeus had a hunger to be whole, to be healed, and nothing was going to get in his way. So his response to those voices, and what ours should be, too, was to cry out even more loudly, "Son of David, have mercy on me!"

When Jesus heard Bartimaeus, he stopped walking and called for Bartimaeus. Even though blind, Bartimaeus sprang up, threw off his cloak, and found his way to Jesus. Bartimaeus was serious about his request for help. He was not just calling on Jesus in vain, waiting to be served – he demonstrated his faith and sincerity by finding his way to Jesus even though he couldn't see.

Jesus knew the struggles Bartimaeus was facing; he could see that Bartimaeus was blind and was poor. But Bartimaeus might also be struggling with something deeper, something spiritual. Bartimaeus might not be concerned with his own physical blindness or poverty as much as he was concerned with his ability to appreciate God's love and know how to live with it. Jesus respected this man and didn't presume he needed help. He asked Bartimaeus, "What do you want me to do for you?"

Bartimaeus asked of Jesus, "My teacher, let me *see* again." Jesus said to him, "Go; your faith has made you well." Bartimaeus' sight returned, and he followed Jesus along the road to Jerusalem.

Many people view this encounter as a healing of Bartimaeus' physical blindness, and this may well be so. But the word "see" also can mean to "understand" or "perceive." It may well be that Bartimaeus simply wanted a deeper insight into life, so that he could better know, love and serve the Lord, regardless of his state in life. He might have realized that his physical blindness and poverty were making him bitter and angry with others. John writes in his first letter, "Whoever hates another person is in the darkness, walks in the darkness, and does not know the way to go, because the darkness has brought on blindness." (1 John 2:11)

Spiritual blindness can be a worse condition than physical blindness. "To open one's eyes" is a phrase used to express understanding or awareness of the truth. In Acts 26, verses 17 and 18, for example, we read about how Jesus was sending Paul to "open people's eyes" so that they may turn from darkness to the Light, from the power of Satan to the power of God.

In Matt. 6, verses 22 and 23, Jesus teaches us that the eye is the lamp of the body. "So, if your eye is healthy, your whole body will be full of Light. But if your eye is unhealthy, your whole body will be full of darkness." As the psalmist of Ps. 146

writes, "The Lord sets the prisoners free; He opens the eyes of the blind." (v. 7, 8)

Bartimaeus set a good example for us. He went to Jesus for help over the objections of opposing voices, humbled himself, and asked for sight. Because of Jesus's love for him, Bartimaeus was once again able to really see, and live the life he was supposed to live.

LUKE 19:1-10
Salvation is a Journey that Begins Now

Zacchaeus, a rich tax collector, felt some deep dissonance within himself, something that persistently disturbed his peace, letting him know that things were not right in his heart. His money didn't satisfy him, and his power didn't satisfy him. He was living a false life, he was living a lie, and he knew it.

Zacchaeus had heard about Jesus, and felt the urge to find out if Jesus could provide an answer. Jesus was coming to Jericho, so Zacchaeus was determined to at least see him. Climbing a tree to get above the crowds, Zacchaeus was stunned when Jesus stopped and invited himself to Zacchaeus's house. Once the encounter with the loving Christ happened, there was no turning back – Zacchaeus was now a changed man, and Jesus proclaimed that "Today salvation has come to this house."

Salvation has a beginning, but perhaps has no end. It becomes a way of life that starts now and continues on through eternity. Salvation means that the past is surrendered to the mercy of God, the future is left to the Providence of God, and the present moment becomes filled with the love of God. There is no room left for anything but the love of God. Each moment becomes a new past, and shapes a new future.

The tugging that Zacchaeus felt in his heart was placed there by God. It won't go away, because God's love for us won't go away. It's steadfast and enduring. It's an invitation to be open to God's love, to His guidance, and to His presence. If we accept this invitation, as Zacchaeus did, we meet God through the living Jesus, and we see in him what we are meant to be.

Salvation is taking the next step to become that person.

What happened to Zacchaeus? He ended up sharing his wealth with the poor. He made restitution for his past wrongs. And he viewed his life very differently from that moment on. He became the person that he was made to be. As Paul wrote in 2 Cor. 5, "A person in Christ is a new creation; everything old has passed away, everything has become new." That is salvation.

Our task is to discover who we were made to be, to become who we really are – not what other people want us to be. We must find our place in the body of Christ, wherever that might be, and realize that whatever it is we're doing, it's equally important to the body as every other part. Read Paul's description of the body of Christ in 1 Cor. 12. He does an excellent job of keeping things in perspective.

The crowds of people (things and pressures of this world) can keep us from seeing this truth, much like the crowds that kept Zacchaeus from seeing Jesus. Zacchaeus separated himself from the crowd so that he had a chance to see the one who would bring him salvation. Find your own sycamore tree and climb it. As the psalmist writes in Ps. 119, "Give me understanding that I may live." (v. 144)

LUKE 19:11-27

The Power of One Talent
(Matt. 25:14-30)

The parable of the talents emphasizes the power of even a single talent – doing something good within our power regardless of how little we think that thing is.

The story opens with a master giving his servants each a talent (a mina, or a sum of money). Assume that these "talents" represent skills, abilities, interests, and opportunities given to each one.

Each person was given some time to use his or her talents for good. This idea represents what happens during our own earthly lifetime – we all have only a certain amount of time to use what we have been given. When the master returned (representing our passing from this life to the next), he asked for an accounting of how the talents were used. If that person used them for good (multiplying their impact), he or she was blessed with, "Well done, good and faithful servant." One of the servants returned ten times the amount, another returned five times the amount.

Then the story turns to the servant who returned only what had been given – one talent. This servant was afraid to use the talent that he had been given, so instead he buried it. No one gained anything from that talent – no good came from it at all.

Not using what we have been given ultimately costs us a great price. We lose our identity, our stability, and our relationships, and darkness gradually overshadows our soul. How better to describe this as "weeping and gnashing of teeth?"

Our merciful God, in good judgment, will consider all the facts of a person's life. One's life situation may greatly inhibit or enhance the ability to use one's talents. Every person's life situation is different – we don't always know what someone else has been through, or what they might be facing at any moment. Many people have been through some horrible things, and that can certainly take its toll on one's attitude toward others.

The challenge here is to improve every present moment with even the smallest act of good. There is always *something* good that can be done in each and every moment we live, regardless of the situation we're in. Certainly, some people have had to live under very oppressive conditions, but there always have been stories of acts of kindness even during the most difficult circumstances, small acts such as sharing pieces of bread, a smile, or a word of encouragement – each with the potential to make a world of difference.

The parable of the talents was crafted to emphasize this personal power – it was not intended to reinforce the idea of an angry or vengeful God. The basic talent we all have is the power of choice over the present moment. It's a power based in love, and manifests itself in many simple ways: a smile, a blessing, time spent listening, acceptance of the moment, sharing a story, admitting a fault, acknowledging a talent in someone else, a gentle touch, a kind word, a friendly note.

What little thing can you do right now, in this moment?

LUKE 19:28-44

Outer Cloaks
(Matt. 21:1-11. Mark 11:1-11. John 12:12-19)

Two themes dominate this reading. The first is the fact that Jesus wanted to make sure people understood that his ministry, his messianic message, was not one of a military conqueror, but a conqueror of the heart. To emphasize this message, he made a "grand entrance" into Jerusalem on the back of a donkey, a small colt, and not with a band of soldiers in chariots brandishing weapons.

Ps. 118, a processional psalm, stresses over and over that the Kingdom of God is based on love, and not on a vindictive God seeking to punish and torture. Again and again, the message in this psalm is "God's steadfast love endures forever!"

God's love is unconditional and unbroken. When humanity sinks to its lowest point and gathers together to execute the very Son of God later in this last week of his ministry, even then God's love doesn't falter. Instead, God embraces the depth of humanity, and conquers death, bringing Jesus back again on Easter morning to prove that nothing can separate us from the love of God. His love is undeniable and invincible.

The second theme in this passage has to do with how we're willing to receive Christ into our lives. An ancient tradition was to lay down an outer cloak at the approach of royalty as an act of homage and respect. As Jesus approached Jerusalem, it was reported that some of his followers" spread their cloaks on the road."

The symbolism of this act can be seen in Paul's letter to the Philippians, where he writes about how Christ "emptied himself," taking on the mind of a servant, and not exploiting his equality with God. Paul was urging us to do this very same thing, "Let the same mind be in you that was in Christ Jesus." (v. 2:5)

In today's terms, this means letting go of what is often called the earthly self, the outer self, the small self, or the dysfunctional ego. This is part of a public image we project out to others; it's how we want other people to see us, even if it's not always the truth of who we really are.

This outer self creates a shell that resists wisdom and instruction from God. It's the part that nurtures unhealthy personality traits like prejudice, fear, shame, bias, greed, envy, and the like. It filters facts to fit what the ego desires, but not what the soul needs.

In the presence of God in Christ we don't need a public image. Our own soul-self, when projected outward, will do just fine. Christ accepts us as we are, regardless of our past or current condition. He only asks that we lay down the false outer shell so that he can be with us and raise us up in love.

That's what the people on the road to Jerusalem were symbolizing. They took off their outer cloaks, representing their false selves, and laid them at the feet of Jesus. What remained was the true self, the self that God made, the self that is interconnected with everyone else. It's the self that can learn about love from God, as Isaiah wrote, "The Lord God has opened my ear, and I was not rebellious (v. 50:5)...he wakens my ear to listen as those who are taught..." (v. 50:4)

What does your outer cloak look like? Will you will it at the feet of Christ?

LUKE 19:45-48

Whac-A-Jesus
(Matt. 21:12-17. Mark 11:15-19. John 2:13-22)

I never thought I could relate the Whac-A-Mole game to Jesus, but after reading this section of the Gospel, it seems to fit. In the game, a mole-like animal pops his head up through any of several holes in a small table. The player, hammer in hand, attempts to whack the mole on the head to get rid of him. Once struck, he pops up again from a different hole. He is persistent, resilient, and never gives up.

That's a lot like Jesus. He was persistent in his ministry – teaching in the temple, on the street, in a house, on a hillside, or from a boat. He popped up in many places, ready to teach, heal, and offer his support. And he was frequently attacked; often verbally at first, then threatened with stoning or being thrown off a cliff. Finally, he was arrested, abused, and crucified. But he never gave up. He returned each and every time to continue his mission – even after the crucifixion!

What kept him going? Where did he get his energy? What was his motivation? Simply put, it was the love of God for His people; a love that endures forever. (Rom. 8:38-39) And it was the people's attraction to this wonderful message – a teaching of equality, equity, unity, and harmony among people – that kept them listening. Often those in power who wanted Jesus out of the way couldn't do anything against him because "all the people hung on his words." Jesus's message went straight to the heart of the soul. He spoke the truth, and the people knew it. Those people with an open heart and mind liked what they heard, and wanted more. Those people whose souls were encrusted in a dysfunctional ego wanted him out of the way.

Late in the day on that Good Friday was not the only time that people have tried to bury Jesus. He has been crucified and buried many times since then in other subtle ways. Some people have tried to bury him in their own busy-ness, illusions and distractions, or in their own weak logic, or simply by ignoring him. Even the Church has occasionally attempted to cover him up with confusing and irrelevant doctrines and rituals that often miss the point of God's love, compassion and mercy.

Regardless of what we do to him, however, he keeps coming at us with his wisdom of love. He won't give up. His love endures forever, and nothing, but nothing, can get in his way – even death on a cross. We whack him down, he turns up somewhere else; persistent, resilient, and loving. The truth will win.

LUKE 20:1-8

The Christian Confession
(Matt. 21:23-27. Mark 11:27-33)

Early in Jesus's ministry, John the Baptist sent two of his own disciples to Jesus to ask him if he was indeed the Messiah that was supposed to come. (John was in prison at the time.) John knew that the Messiah was to be a Messiah of the soul, not of the sword as most people thought. "Are you he that is to come, or do we look for another?" the two disciples asked. Jesus answered them, not with claims or argument, but with the fruits of his ministry. "Show John those things which you hear and see: the blind receive their sight, the lepers are cleansed, the deaf hear, the dead are raised, and the poor have the gospel preached to them." (Matt. 11:3-5)

John welcomed the arrival of the Messiah, but there were others that feared his arrival, whether he was a Messiah of the sword or of the heart. The Messiah, people believed, would come to release the Jewish people from the oppression they were under, but would also significantly change the current power structure and those enjoying its benefits. Those in power at the time evolved into a collective dysfunctional ego that fed their illusion of status, provided them with material benefits, and afforded them some privileges not available to everyone else.

When the leaders (the chief priests, scribes, and elders) heard about Jesus, they were naturally concerned that his ministry could cause an uprising among the people that would endanger the delicate relationship they had with the Roman authorities. This uprising could lead to the collapse of whatever the leaders had left of their own authority and power. So they challenged Jesus and hoped that he would fall into a trap that could lead to his arrest and prosecution – and, if necessary, his death.

While Jesus was teaching in the temple, they came to him and demanded, "Tell us, by what authority do you do these things? Who gave you this authority?"

Jesus knew the trap. It was very difficult, if not impossible, to claim any authority through personal acclamation or by scriptural argument. He had to turn the tables on these egos without playing their game. So, using good rabbinical technique, he answered their question with a question: "Was the baptism ministry of John from heaven, or of men?"

In other words, Jesus was asking them whether John's ministry was a work of God that spread God's love, or was

John doing this to serve his own ego? The answer should have been obvious. John's work was bringing people to God. It was evident in the fruits of his labor – the commitment of hundreds, if not thousands, or people to God through their baptism.

Now the leaders were trapped in their own game. If they agreed that the work of John was from God, then Jesus would ask them, "Then why didn't you believe him?" But if they said that what John did was for his own good, the people would rise up against them because the people knew it was indeed God at work in their hearts.

"You shall know them by their fruits," Jesus reminded us. (Matt. 7:16-20) John knew that Jesus was "the one who was to come," not because Jesus claimed he was the Messiah, but because Jesus *demonstrated* he was the Messiah. He healed, he taught, he comforted, he loved.

We can easily claim we are Christians, but that doesn't make us Christians. To be Christian, we need to build a life around the Gospel truth. We need to build a life of prayer – prayers of gratitude, prayers of intercession, prayers of listening, and prayers of healing. We need to discover our true selves, and learn how to dissolve any bits of the false self that still cling to us – those things that block the natural goodness that God put into each of us. Then, as we learn what skills, interests and talents we've been given, we use them to serve that little corner of the world we've found ourselves in. "How can I be of help in this moment, where I am right now, even in the simplest way?" The smallest acts of service are huge in the eyes of God – a smile, a silent blessing, feeding a bird, holding a door for someone, picking up a nail off the street – if it's an act of love, it's an act of service to God whether someone sees it or not.

We confess we are Christ's by becoming Christ's.

LUKE 20:9-19

The Tenants will be Healed
(Matt. 21:33-46. Mark 12:1-12)

The parable of the vineyard and its wicked tenants has been used as an allegory to describe the kingdom of God. A certain man (God) planted a vineyard (the earth) and rented it out to some tenants (while the early Church believed this was the Jews, it probably better applies to all of us). Later, God sent some servants (prophets) to the vineyard to collect some of the harvest. But the tenants continued to abuse these prophets, and refused to listen to them. Finally, God sent His beloved Son (Jesus Christ), whom the tenants dragged from the vineyard and murdered.

What's the owner to do? Should he "come and destroy those tenants, and give the vineyard to others"? The answer from the crowd was, "God forbid!"

Jesus went on to explain the situation more clearly. He used the verse Ps. 118:22, "The very stone which the builders rejected has become the cornerstone." This Stone, Christ himself, would be a cleansing stone. It will preserve the good parts within each tenant, but will indeed destroy the bad parts. It is the cornerstone of the Kingdom, a kingdom of renewal, regeneration, and reconciliation.

Verse 18 describes how this will work: "Everyone who falls on that stone will be broken to pieces, but when it falls on anyone it will crush him."

As we work in our own vineyard, the place where we've been planted in life, we might come across the Presence of God in Christ along the way. We might have been looking for this Presence, or we might have accidentally stumbled upon this

Stone, but in either case, we are in for some major changes in our lives, because whoever falls upon this Stone "will be broken."

It's not a bad brokenness, but instead a separation of our true selves from our false selves. He will help us realize the false attachments and illusions that have directed our lives and have been making decisions for us. It is, as one parable puts it, separating our wheat (the good parts) from the chaff (the not-so-good parts). And the "ungodly" parts of us, the chaff, are blown away by the wind – the Holy Spirit. (Ps. 1:4) All the prejudices, sadness, arrogance, greed, fear, shame, inferiority, self-pride, and other scales that were covering our eyes gradually fall away to reveal the true, natural goodness in our hearts and souls. The broken pieces are reassembled into a true human being.

Some people avoid encountering the Stone during their lifetime, preferring instead to live within their illusions. Their dysfunctional ego has totally encapsulated them, and they have become spiritually blind. Their egos will do anything to survive, even to the detriment of themselves. But the love this Stone has will never cease, and at some point, it will "fall" on them. There is no escape. The transformation will happen in these cases, too, but the person may resist and deny the change with every ounce of their being. The appearance of Christ in their lives will be a crushing blow, at least at first until they, too, begin to see God's eternal love and truth.

It's God's plan to bring everyone of His children home to Him, healthy and whole. No one will be left behind. Whether we seek to find Him, or He comes after us, it will happen, either in this life or the next. This is God's justice – reconciliation and restoration – not punishment and retribution.

LUKE 20:20-26

Caesar's Currency
(Matt. 22:15-22. Mark 12:13-17)

Pretending to be supporters of Jesus, spies were sent by the chief priests and scribes in an attempt to trap him into a crime that would get him arrested. They tried to win him over first by saying, "Master, we know that what you teach and say is right, and what you say comes from God and not the authority from any person. So tell us, is it lawful to give tribute to Caesar or not?"

Their excessive gushing triggered a caution in Jesus. "Why do you tempt me?" he demanded.

Then Jesus asked to see a coin, and asked whose image and inscription was on it. "Caesar's," they replied. Jesus responded with the well-known line, "Then render unto Caesar the things that are Caesar's, and unto God the things that are God's."

Jesus neatly avoided the trap, and in doing so, left us with an important insight into life. There are two realms at play in our life. One, of course, is the kingdom of God which beckons our heart and soul. The other is mankind's world which appeals to things of the mind and ego. It's the age-old struggle between the heart and the head, and these two realms are often at odds with each other. They have different goals and different purposes, and their currencies are very different. While mankind's coins have the head of Caesar, God's coins show the heart of love, mercy and compassion.

Isaiah describes the difference between these two realms: "'For my thoughts are not your thoughts, neither are your ways my ways,' says the Lord." (Isa. 55:8) And yet, for now at least, the two must co-exist, occupying the same time and space.

So the trick is to live in mankind's world while practicing the tools and methods of God's world. To live in the world without being a part of (mankind's) world. It's a delicate balance. But the wisdom that Jesus brought to us, and that is recorded in the Gospels, is the key to this balance. At just about every turn Jesus teaches how to live in God's kingdom, while still living in the midst of mankind's world. And we are guided by the ultimate goal as presented in the Lord's Prayer, "Thy kingdom come, Thy will be done, on earth as it is in heaven."

We must work to shape worldly systems to better serve the kingdom so they are in better alignment with the teachings of God. We must continually work to change the negative aspects of these systems, maintaining a constant vigilance against the harm they can cause. We must learn to sort out the good from the bad, retaining what works, and removing or changing what doesn't. This takes wisdom, persistence, patience, awareness and a keen sensitivity.

Here's a great spot for the Serenity Prayer! Remember it every day upon awakening. One version goes like this:

> *Lord, Grant me the Serenity to accept*
> *the things I cannot change,*
> *The courage to change the things I can,*
> *And the wisdom to know the difference.*

It's not easy to live in a world with opposing systems. There is constant pressure to surrender to mankind's systems, which can be draining. So it's also important to strike a balance between our time in the world, and our time alone with God. Our "downtime" in prayer, meditation, sleep, rest, and contemplation will help us to recharge our spiritual batteries, regain our focus, and renew our connections with the kingdom of God.

LUKE 20:27-40

Are Marriages Made in Heaven?
(Matt. 22:23-33. Mark 12:18-27)

The Sadducees were part of a Jewish religious group active during the time of Jesus's ministry. They were associated with the upper social and economic classes of the time, and managed the Temple activities. They generally didn't believe in the resurrection of the body, or even that a person had a soul, and therefore sometimes clashed with Jesus.

In Luke 20 we encounter another example of this. They challenged Jesus again, this time pressing him with a somewhat sarcastic question about marriage in the afterlife. They asked him about a woman who married seven times in her earthly life and, after her earthly death, "Whose wife shall she be in the resurrection?"

Jesus squashed their challenge with a simple response stating that marriage was a human institution, and not something needed in the time of resurrection. It's something people do in this life, but not in the next. Why? Because in the next life we will all be considered brothers and sisters – children of the one God – and won't be marrying anyone. It just won't be necessary.

Marriage is indeed a human institution, and took many forms throughout history. Even today there are many types of marriage. Some cultures allow polygamous marriage, and some allow same-sex marriages. In some cultures, marriages are arranged by force. Other marriages are created to simply designate who belongs to whom, as one would hold title to property. Many cultures prohibit marriages between close relatives for genetic reasons. Others simply arrange them for political reasons or for succession of property.

Jesus was not diminishing the value of a good marriage when he answered the Sadducees. In fact, he knew that good marriages add to a culture, and serve to strengthen a society, not to mention the value it can have for an immediate family.

But Jesus *was* trying to keep things in perspective, considering the much larger marriage occurring between God and all His children, bringing them into His family. This is a marriage of our spirits – our souls – a blessed union that lasts forever. By pointing this out to the Sadducees, he was also emphasizing that people do, indeed, have souls. His exclamation point to the Sadducees was, "God is not God of the dead, but of the living; for to Him all of them are alive."

It would benefit all of us if we could start viewing ourselves in this life as the brothers and sisters we'll be in the next. It has always been God's intent to bring His kingdom to earth, and that's what we pray for when we offer the Lord's Prayer: "Thy kingdom come, Thy will be done, on earth as it is in heaven."

If a marriage here on Earth can bring two people (any two people) closer to God, and helps these two people build a loving relationship with each other (which, in turn, helps them to learn how to love their neighbors), then we're stepping out of bounds if we stand in their way. It is, after all, a small reflection of a much bigger family reunion that is coming soon!

How much would this world change if we could greet each other as a family member?

LUKE 20:41-47

The Hypocrisy of the Ego
(Matt. 22:41-46; 23:1-36. Mark 12:35-40)

One of the most troublesome things for Jesus was mankind's hypocrisy (which he found quite frequently in some of the scribes and Pharisees). This hypocrisy was borne of an overpowering ego that grew like algae over one's heart. It fed the false self that was clearly visible to everyone but its owners; the extravagant clothing they wore, the undue attention they demanded from others, and the positions of honor they claimed in the synagogues and at public feasts.

It wasn't the inner true self of these people that Jesus despised. He loves the soul of every person, but not the outer image, the false self that destroys what that person was really made to be. It ends up hurting not only the person it possesses, but causes harm to others as well.

Jesus never attacked the soul of the other person, but would always try to use the power of awareness to expose his or her dysfunctional ego to the Light of Love. Many of the "demons" Jesus exorcised were actually egos that had grown so powerful that they totally possessed the afflicted soul. Bringing them to the Light of Awareness caused them to melt away.

In this episode of Luke, Jesus exposed the true shallowness of the scribe's knowledge when he asked them a question about the nature of the Messiah in the front of a group of people. How could the Messiah be both of David's lineage *and* David's Lord? Jesus fit that description, being a physical descendent of David, and yet a Holy Incarnation of God.

Then Jesus told the crowd what hypocrisy looked like: "Beware of the scribes, who desire to walk in long robes, and love greetings in the markets, and the highest seats in the synagogues, and the chief rooms at feasts; and then devour widow's houses, and for a show make long prayers…"

I can only imagine that this piercing truth brought some embarrassment and humiliation to those scribes who hearts were still accessible. Perhaps it moved them to deep reflection and self-examination. People in the crowd may have enjoyed this exchange between Jesus and the scribes, easily seeing the hypocrisy in some of the scribes who couldn't see it in themselves. But it served as a lesson for everyone, too, to be careful of the fertile ground for the ego that can result from too much power and greed.

Jesus's words probably brought anger to some of the scribes – especially to those whose hearts were hardened tight. This anger joined with other community leaders who furthered their plan to rid themselves of this irritant preacher. A mob mentality soon formed that focused their hatred on this one man. All of these collective egos plotted false charges that would soon lead to a public execution.

LUKE 21:1-4

Of Widows and Sons
(Mark 12:41-44)

Just a few days before his arrest, Jesus sat down for a rest in the shade of a building opposite the temple treasury and watched people depositing money into the treasury box to support the work of the temple. With full attention, he listened to the clanking metal coins going into the box. Many rich people put in large sums, which made a lot of noise. But then a poor widow came by and dropped in two small copper coins. Her actions almost moved Jesus to tears.

It was another teaching moment. After a thoughtful pause, Jesus got the attention of his disciples and said, "Truly I tell you, this poor widow has put in more than all those who are contributing to the treasury. For all of them have contributed out of their abundance; but she out of her poverty has put in everything she had, all she had to live on."

This incident is often used to explain the importance of giving with the heart, and that the gift which counts is the gift which costs. True giving, many teachers would say, is measured relative to what one has to give, not strictly by the size of the gift.

While all of this has merit for discussion, I can't help think that this incident cut deeper into Jesus's heart because of what he would soon face – an arrest, a slanted trial, and a public execution. What else might have been going through his mind when he saw the poor widow giving up something so needed and precious?

Jesus was followed in his last few days of ministry by another widow about to give up something very dear and precious to her. Jesus's mother, now a widow, had a growing sense of what was about to befall her son. Perhaps Jesus saw some deep symbolism in the poor widow walking up to the establishment, the system in power, and surrendering her precious two copper coins – Jesus and Christ, God and man.

Jesus was saddened by what his mother Mary would have to endure in the days ahead. She would lose her son. The gift was everything that Mary had – the price to be paid into the treasury for the good of the whole world. "Truly I tell you, this poor widow has put in more than all those who are contributing to the treasury," reflected Jesus over his impending fate.

But now there was no turning back. Jesus's message of love and compassion threatened too many people in power; it challenged the collective egos that had a grip on society; it provided access to a loving God for everyone; it turned the world upside down.

The appearance of Jesus on earth united spiritual graces with human frailties, creating a family of God on earth that revealed our connections with each other. We are not alone, we are not separate, and we are not disconnected individuals. We are brothers and sisters, children of God, and nothing can separate us from the love of God.

Those who insist we are alone and separate, in this fight for life by ourselves, are living a great delusion. Many of the best minds down through the ages have also realized this. They recognize the importance of Jesus's message about unity, compassion for each other, and our role in nature.

> "A human being is part of a whole, called by the universe, a part limited in time and space. He experiences himself, his thoughts and feelings, as something separated from the rest, a kind of optical delusion of his consciousness. This delusion is a kind of prison for us, restricting us to our personal desires and to affection for a few persons nearest us. Our task must be to free ourselves from this prison by widening our circles of compassion to embrace all living creatures and the whole of nature in its beauty."
>
> Albert Einstein, 1921

Know that the Good Lord loves you very much, unqualified and unconditionally. Take this love and grow in it, and let it flow from you out to others.

LUKE 21:5-24
When Kingdoms Collide
(Matt. 24:1-21. Mark 13:1-19)

The presence of God's love and wisdom in this world has always created tension at some level. Even Jesus said that his arrival here would bring trouble: "Don't think that peace follows me to earth; it's not peace that comes, but a sword." (Matt. 10:34) This is not what someone might imagine would happen upon the arrival of the Lamb of God, the Great Shepherd. But even for him, this tension resulted in his execution on the cross.

So, why is there such tension in the world even today? We find the core of the answer in Isaiah, where he writes, "And God said, 'For my thoughts are not your thoughts, neither are your ways my ways. For as the heavens are higher than the earth, so are my ways higher than your ways, and my thoughts than your thoughts.'" (Isa. 55:8-9)

God is love, and God creates out of love. God wants us to be loving, too. But love can only exist when it's a choice, and that means there must be free will to make that choice. With free will, however, comes the possibility that bad choices will be made – choices that stem from things that cloud the soul, things that are not of God.

Many of mankind's social, economic, political, and religious systems are based on bad choices. As a result, we end up with poverty, famine, diseases, unfair discrimination, economic inequality, waste, wars, and pollution. Some people benefit greatly at the expense of others by creating the power to nurture these lopsided conditions. But these systems are sustained only when those controlling them maintain the power to do so.

Change begins to happen when those who are oppressed are empowered to act.

This is where the tension emerges. Those in power who do not want change to happen strongly oppose those that want the change. Current power structures are threatened; those in power could lose prestige, wealth, power, and visibility (all things of the dysfunctional ego). So they fight back, not realizing what the truth really is. It turns into a battle between egos versus hearts.

Jesus brought us a message of love that was welcomed by many people but despised by others. Ultimately, his opponents arranged a sham trial and had him executed. But, as we know, even that didn't stop him from promoting God's love. And it shouldn't stop us either! As Jesus stated in Luke 21, "You may be hated by all because of my Name. But not a hair of your head will perish. By your endurance you will gain your souls."

Regardless of what happens to us, "all will be well," as Julian of Norwich reminds us. We may suffer some trials and tribulations, but in the end, God will bring us to complete restoration and refreshment in His kingdom.

As Jesus and his disciples walked past the temple, "adorned with beautiful stones and gifts dedicated to God," Jesus predicted that not one of the stones will be left upon another – all would be thrown down. This idea led to a description of what we often think of as the "end times." Perhaps the end times are the final period of change, when Christ returns to establish what Isaiah calls "new heavens and a new earth." (Isa. 65:17) The eternal tension between mankind and God comes to a final resolution, and a new world order is instituted for all our good for all time.

But we don't know when these end times will be. Meantime, we have work to do here. We must continue to fight the good fight of love. And the best way to do this is to become the person you were truly meant to be, and to live your life to its fullest.

Each of us has been given some special gifts, talents, interests, and skills. Our main task is to find out what these are, and then use them to our fullest. Each person contributes to the overall good of God's plan, regardless of what he or she does, as long as it's being who were truly were made to be. We must learn to appreciate gifts not only in ourselves, but in others as well. Just because we have differences does not mean some are better and some are worse. They are all important to God!

Did you know that stopping to admire the beauty of a flower, or to appreciate its fragrance, is creating admiration and appreciation in this world? This is a wonderful creative gift that some people have!

Did you know that offering someone a smile or a kind word strengthens the invisible connections we have between each other, thus creating a stronger family of God? How powerful this talent of creation is!

Did you know that offering a prayer for someone else can actually create a new life in that person (or even in yourself)! The Kingdom grows stronger through this gift!

Don't measure your gifts and skills based on mankind's standards. Remember that God's ways are higher than our ways.

LUKE 21:25-38

O Come, O Come, Emmanuel!
(Matt. 24:29-35. Mark 13:24-31)

The new Church year begins with an ancient promise: "I will cause a Righteous Branch to spring up for David; and he shall bring justice and righteousness in the land." (Jer. 33:15) This promise reflects God's master plan for all of His people, for all time.

We celebrate the coming of this 'Righteous Branch,' both in Jesus the man and in Christ the Risen God. He came to us as the incarnate God two thousand years ago to teach us, to heal us, to be with us, and to show us how to love; he comes to each of us in our own lives, to abide with us as the loving Holy Spirit, and he will come to us again, to complete his reign over everything.

Past, present, and future – all wrapped up like a Christmas present with the same purpose and message – that you "increase and abound in love for one another and for all..." (1 Thess. 3)

We learn of Jesus in the first Christmas story, born in a manger in Bethlehem. We know that he will come again, in full power and glory for the entire world to witness. And we know that he can be welcomed into our own lives today, at this moment.

Every Advent season is a time of acceptance and renewal. It is a time for us to prepare our hearts and minds to accept Jesus into our lives right now, to renew our relationship with him, and to allow him to continue to transform our lives.

How can we open ourselves to this loving power?

The first way comes right out of Luke 21: "Be on guard so that your hearts are not weighed down with dissipation (distractions, lack of focus, being pulled in too many directions) and drunkenness (certainly with drink, but also with power, position, or any of the dysfunctional attachments), and worries of this life..." God teaches us that all will be well, so be alert to the fears generated by social programming that attempt to control your life.

All these things are the 'enemies' we face. People down through the ages have faced many of the same enemies. Psalmists often write about their enemies, and they are not always talking about the soldiers lined up on the other side of the river with swords drawn, waiting to attack. Some of the worst enemies we have are in our heads, because they keep us from receiving God into our hearts – prejudice, arrogance, greed, self-pride, worry, shame, inferiority, and fear, for example.

"Do not let my enemies exult over me," writes the psalmist in Psalm 25:2. How can we be on guard against these enemies? How can we learn to think, speak and behave in the right way?

God sends His Holy Spirit to instruct us in a number of ways. He teaches us through scripture, through Church traditions, through preachers and teachers of the Word, and through life experiences. We also learn from Him through our friends and spiritual directors, through our encounters with Him in prayer and meditation, and through the promptings of the Holy Spirit as the conscience in our hearts.

The distractions of this life tend to keep us too busy to spend time with God. Christmas is a reminder that God loves us and wants to be a part of our lives. It is a time to look closely at our lives, to realize that maybe God wants us not to be so busy, but to spend some more time with Him – reading the Bible, praying to Him, praying for all people, feeling the joy of His presence, and looking carefully at all His wonders that He has given us every day because He loves us.

Christmas is a loving gift to us from God, the Righteous Branch promised to us so long ago.

LUKE 22:1-6

The Tipping Point
(Matt. 26:1-5, 14, 16. Mark 14:1, 2, 10, 11. John 11:45-53)

It was near the end of Jesus's ministry, not because he wanted it to end, but because his enemies were now plotting to have him killed. Jesus was making an impression on many people. Some found his message to their liking, and others decided it was too dangerous.

Jesus's teaching of love, compassion, and mercy fostered ideas of equality, inclusiveness, and fairness for all people. This was an attractive message to those whose hearts were open and were looking for a better way to live together.

But it was also a very threatening message to those who enjoyed their powerful positions and authority, whose true selves were encapsulated by dysfunctional egos that tightened the grip around lost hearts and minds. When Jesus was not well known, he was not a problem. He could be ignored. But now he had a strong following, and it was turning into a movement. What if he *was* the Messiah? Then things would be different, and those in power could very well be replaced by someone else. Even if Jesus was a Messiah of the heart, this could also cause a serious disruption in the status quo, and cause trouble with the Roman occupiers. There was too much risk, so he had to go.

Jesus had some measure of protection because he had a strong following. So those out to dispose of him had to find a way to do so when Jesus was away from his supporters. The turning point came when the Jewish Council was approached by Judas Iscariot.

It's likely that Judas was expecting Jesus to be the military Messiah foretold in scriptures and tradition. Perhaps Judas expected to be an important part of the new command, marshalling power and authority as one of the twelve apostles. But now, as the Passover drew near, Judas realized that Jesus was to be a Messiah of the heart, not of the sword. Jesus's ministry was designed to change the world from the inside out, not the outside in.

Judas's ego got the better of him. It was described in Luke as, "Satan entered into Judas." He was totally possessed by his dysfunctional ego – he completely identified with his illusion. He would be denied the role that he expected to play in the new political order. He might have felt much betrayed by Jesus, having spent so many months under Jesus's leadership with the expectation of having greater power. Since he felt betrayed by Jesus, why should he not, in turn, betray Jesus?

So Judas "went away and conferred with the chief priests and scribes" as to how he could betray Jesus to them. A deal was struck, and the plan was set into motion. Whether or not this betrayal was a predestined Christological necessity in the grand scheme of things can be left to the theologians to debate – but there is no question that it could have been predicted. The Gospel of John records that Jesus knew that Judas was troubled, and would most likely betray him at some point. (John 6:70-71)

LUKE 22:7-13

The Mission Must Go On
(Matt. 26:17-25. Mark 14:12-21. John 13:21-30)

In the midst of betrayal and at the doorstep of death, Jesus still moves ahead with plans to celebrate the Passover with his disciples and friends. Honoring the traditions of his people, he sends Peter and John ahead to prepare for the Passover soon to arrive.

The Passover celebrated the Hebrews initial release from the bonds of oppression at the hands of the ancient Egyptians. The wisdom of Jesus can release us, too, from the bonds of oppression that enslave us – things that encapsulate our true selves, things that over-inflate our sense of self-worth, or even those things that debase our own self-esteem. When we lose sight of our true self, we begin to identify with things not of God. We become imprisoned by our attachments.

Becoming aware that our mind is not a part of our true self is just the beginning of our journey. Our mind is meant to serve us, not to control us. There will still be good times and bad, times when we doubt the presence of God, and times when we celebrate His involvement in our lives.

Jesus's mission was to awaken us to the power of love, and how it can release us from the bonds of the mind. To become who we were meant to be would change not only our own lives, but would ultimately change the world as well. It would bring the kingdom of God to Earth.

There was nothing more important for him to do for us, even if it meant his own death. He was willing to sacrifice his own life to make sure that as much of this message of love would reach us as possible. He would not give up, he would not be deterred. This innocent Son of God would die at the hands of the very thing he was trying to cure – the collective dysfunctional egos that bring darkness to the world.

Would Jesus die *for* our sins, or *because* of them? Did God send Jesus to Earth to die as a payment for some cosmic debt owed to Him? Would a loving, all-powerful, compassionate God need to have this blood of His own Son? If Jesus would die to pay for all the sins of the world, why is there still so much sinning going on?

Perhaps the sacrifice Jesus made for us was to devote his entire life to his mission, even at the risk of his own death. He gave up all other choices, took no other direction, but spent every second he had in preparing and delivering his message from God because he knew it was the most important thing that could ever be done for mankind. He didn't have to come to earth to teach us and heal us and show us the way to life – he came to us because he loved us dearly.

The cost of making poor choices as a free-willed human being was revealed to us in the story of Adam and Eve. It is a story about all of us, and the power of choice that we've all been given. Jesus, the second Adam, was sent to teach us how to live with this power of choice, and why we need to make the right choices. Look around! Can you see what happens in the world when bad choices are made? This is why we need to listen to Jesus's wisdom. This is why the message he brought to us is so important, and why he wouldn't stop his ministry at any cost. This is the salvation that he brings to us if we follow it.

His blood spills when we reject his wisdom, as we saw on the cross – the ultimate example of our folly. His broken body on the cross would represent the lowest point to which humans can fall. Hopefully that would serve as a reminder to awaken!

LUKE 22:14-23

The Last Supper
(Matt. 26:26-30. Mark 14:22-26)

It's my understanding that there was an old Eastern custom that when someone was about to go on a long journey, he would gather his friends together before his departure, and serve them a meal as a symbol of his enduring love for them. He prepared the table, and told his friends to take the food and eat it. Regardless of the distance that would be separating them, the bread they ate would make their bodies as though one body, and the wine they drank would be the same lifeblood that kept them all alive. Never would they really be apart from one another, as they only had to look into their hearts to find each other.

This type of gathering seems to be the context within which Jesus offered his last meal, the event we know as the Last Supper. He, too, was about to depart, to go to a place where the others could not go. But he wanted to assure them that even though separated in body, he would be one with them in their hearts.

"This is my body, given for you..." he offered, "Take it and eat, in remembrance of me." The bread of heaven unites us with the Son of God in an intimate and permanent union. He abides in us, and we in him. We eat the same bread, this manna, and remember that we are, indeed, part of the body of Christ. Each of us is an important member; each of us different and yet the same. A common purpose fulfilled in unique ways.

In his body rests a common heart, filled with the conscious desire to be in harmony with God, to serve in joy. We are the hands of God, doing the work of God. We are His feet, taking us to where we are needed within the boundaries of our life; and we His eyes, seeing the world in its beauty, and looking for ways to spread His love.

But what brings this body to life? What blood flows through its veins and arteries to nourish each of its cells, giving them strength and power?

"Jesus took the cup of wine in his hands and gave thanks to God… Drink this, all of you, as a testament of my love for you." This is the cup of salvation, the lifeblood of the body, which nourishes all who drink from it. It's what makes the body come alive in love. It's the wisdom and power bestowed upon us by the Holy Spirit. It's the blood that keeps the entire body alive, flowing with the presence and companionship of God, making us truly all one Holy Communion.

This farewell meal became a sacramental cornerstone of Christian belief. It's a meal of promise and hope. A promise that we do not walk alone, but rather in unity with all of God's children. A reminder, as often as we partake in it, that we are forever safe in the arms of God, and the hope that we will one day return to Him with tears of joy.

This meal refreshes and renews, reminding us how we are supposed to live together. When we share a meal together, invisible walls of fear and uncertainty dissolve away. We allow a natural festivity to emerge, filling our hearts with the joy of being all the same body of Christ. It's not a committee or a team, but a *body* working in unison for a common good. It's the body and blood of Christ.

LUKE 22:24-30

Service with a Secret
(Mark 9:33-35)

When the scent of power and privilege reaches the nose of mankind, the ego often rouses from its sleep to prepare for a coming feast. The desire to take advantage of an opportunity to acquire prestige and control is a natural, but overinflated, result of a deeply imbedded self-preservation instinct. We all want to survive, and in our primitive state we'll grasp at whatever is available to secure our advantage over another. To have this power and privilege makes us feel more important than others, and thereby strengthens our sense of preservation.

Some of the disciples thought that this opportunity would present itself soon, especially as they sensed that Jesus was rising to higher-level authority in his coming kingdom. Who will be the greatest of Jesus's followers? Can I sit at your right hand, Lord? Will it be me?

It's true, responded Jesus, that in most of mankind's systems "kings exercise leadership over others, and those in authority over them are called benefactors." But as he's done so many times before, Jesus was careful to point out the difference between mankind's systems and God's kingdom: "But not so with you; rather let the greatest among you become as the youngest [often getting the worst of the chores], and the leader as the one who serves."

Once again Jesus flips our current understanding upside down. "You see," he explained, "in mankind's system the one who sits at the table is greater than the one who serves." But in God's kingdom, it's the opposite – "I am among you as one who serves."

LUKE 22:31-38

When You Have Turned Again...
(Matt. 26:31-35. Mark 14:27-31. John 13:36-38)

There will always be failures, but never total failure.

Jesus knew that his disciples would fail him at the crucial moment. He told Peter directly that he would deny Jesus three times the night Jesus was arrested, even though Peter insisted that he would be willing to die with Jesus.

But Jesus knew that his disciples would eventually recover from their fall, and would go on to serve him the rest of their lives. He said to Peter, "When you have turned again, be sure to help the others." When you have turned again...It's almost as though Jesus is forgiving him in advance of his denial! He knows the human spirit. He knows that living this life is not easy, and that we are bound to fall every once in a while. This isn't an excuse for wayward behavior, but it offers us the assurance that God is understanding and compassionate. He doesn't want us to fall, but we need to know that just because we do, it's not the gateway to eternal damnation. He is there, waiting to help us get back up again, and then continue on our journey.

We all slip and fall, because we are part human; we can get up again, if we are willing, because we are part spirit. The union of our flesh and spirit still leaves some gaps and holes that can only be filled with the Presence of God. God is the mortar that cements the spirit to the flesh, filling all the cracks and open places that need this vital glue.

The Presence of God in us is a prayer that our faith will be strong. It's an assurance that we *can* get back up again, and when we are ready, to continue on our journey.

LUKE 22:39-46
Why Did Jesus Have to Die?
(Matt. 26:36-46. Mark 14:32-42)

The last supper with his disciples was finished, and Jesus walked out into the night air, deeply burdened with the events soon to come. He needed strength and reassurance, so it was time to pray. He had a special place on the Mount of Olives he had been to before, a place of peace and serenity where he could reconnect with the Father. His disciples followed along as they always had, but they would soon scatter from the evil that approached in the dark. Judas was already busy completing his plans of betrayal while Jesus went off alone to recommit to God's will.

Jesus asked the Father to be relieved of what was about to happen: "Father if you are willing, remove this cup from me…" Jesus had a sense of what was to happen, and his natural humanness would prefer to avoid it if there were another way. Wouldn't we all?

But there was something higher to be considered – the overall will of God. Jesus concluded his request with, "…nevertheless, not my will, but Yours, be done." And here we crash into some deep theological issues. Was this really the will of God that Jesus should go through this torture, humiliation and agonizing death? Is this the act of a loving God? Isn't God smart enough to figure out some other way to stop all this insanity? Was it preordained that Jesus must die for the sin of Adam? Does God really demand a divine sacrifice to pay for original sin?

Philosophers, theologians, and antagonists have grappled with this fundamental issue for two thousand years. While it's a settled issue for some, it's a continuing enigma for others. Each person has to decide what answer works best for him or her. My understanding of this issue rests on the fact that love is a choice, and therefore requires free will to choose it.

First of all, God is love, and God wishes us to love, too. But since love is a choice (or it could not be love at all) there has to be free will to choose it. But it's a risky business. We can use this free will to perform loving acts and thoughts, or we can use it in selfish ways that serve our own interests. The symbols of Adam and Eve represent each one of us when we let our serpent ego get the better of us and we make bad choices with our free will.

But the serpent ego isn't something to be punished – it's something to be healed. Our dysfunctional egos can be healed through awareness, forgiveness, understanding, guidance, compassion, companionship, and values. We grow into our spiritual maturity by reconnecting with God. Hebrew Scriptures, the New Testament, and the writing of spiritual seekers down through the ages have offered ways to awaken and grow spiritually. The capstone of this instruction, and reconnecting of spirit with flesh, is through the incarnation of God's Son, Jesus.

I don't believe that God's plan included a demand of Jesus's life in exchange for our original sin (the capacity to use our free will in bad ways). The Divine Plan was for God to come down to Earth to be with the people He dearly loved, to teach them, and to heal them, and to be with them. "For God so loved the world that He sent His only begotten Son that whosoever believe on him would have an eternal life and never really die. God did not send His Son into the world to condemn it, but to save it." (John 3:16-17)

Yes, there was the risk that Jesus's presence on Earth could inflame the already distorted egos of those in power at the time. Something bad could happen – and did. Jesus was ultimately killed by the collective dysfunctional egos of the time, but not as a Divine sacrifice to pay for some cosmic debt. It was not God's will that Jesus had to suffer a humiliating and painful death. But it was God's will that Jesus make every attempt to deliver this message of love, compassion and mercy.

Jesus's death came about because his message and ministry was toxic to those who stood the most to lose by it; it was quite predictable that serious action would be taken against Jesus at some point. He died to make sure that we got the wisdom we needed. He gave his life in his effort to heal us, teach us, and show us how to live. Some people reject this love, and other people embrace it.

In today's world, God's involvement can be seen in many ways: people speaking out against injustices and inequality, street protests, voting with ballots and with our dollars, emergency relief efforts, homeless shelters, food pantries, support groups, twelve-step programs, counselors, doctors, therapists, and many non-profit organizations created to help others. God is very busy!

LUKE 22:47-53

The Power of Free Will
(Matt. 26:47-56. Mark 14:43-50. John 18:3-11)

There are times when evil seems to prevail. Jesus, praying in the garden, was now surrounded by people determined to harm him. The signs of evil in this encounter are easily noticed; the betrayer uses a kiss to reveal the betrayed, violence swells up in the hearts of those present, mob mentality rules the moment, and night is used to hide evil intentions.

Jesus had power to walk on water, turn water into wine, cure the sick, and raise the dead, but he didn't resist the advances of his attackers. Why? Because his power was limited against free-will choices. Even during his ministry, when Jesus met people who had no faith in his works, he was unable to heal or teach. He would go elsewhere. And here, against a mob determined to arrest him, he knew resistance would be futile.

Why is free will choice so powerful, even to the point that Jesus succumbed to it?

It all goes back to the fact that free will is a necessary condition for love to exist. Love is a choice, and therefore requires the ability to choose it. If it were not a choice, then it couldn't be love. Robots can't love. The ability to choose love means that there has to be free will to choose it. But free will is also a risk, because free will can also be used to choose evil.

Bringing swords and clubs, the crowd came prepared to use force to arrest Jesus if necessary. They had made up their mind. Reacting to the threat of the crowd, a disciple drew his sword and cut the ear of one of the attackers. An escalation of violence was inevitable. Jesus saw this, and he stopped its progression by shouting, "No more of this!" Although he couldn't stop mankind's free will decisions, he still had the power to heal, so he touched the wounded man's ear and healed it. Jesus did what he was able to do in a tense situation driven by human free will.

People can certainly make their own choices, as we all know. But they can't choose their own consequences. I can choose to jump off a building, but I can't stop gravity from performing as it should. The extent of my injuries will be governed by the laws of physics, not my free will.

The development of free will (so that it helps us make good choices) is based on a number of variables: our training as a child, our value systems, the advice we get before making a decision, the strength of our consciences, and so on. The key ingredient is having a strong tie to our true selves, and therefore a connection with our spiritual roots. Even Carl Jung, the famous psychologist, stated that when a person gets further and further from the laws and roots of his or her being, he or she may experience more perceived freedom, but will also create the possibility of "endless transgressions." (*The Archetypes and the Collective Unconscious,* The Collected Works of C. G. Jung, Volume 9, Part 1, p.163)

To know how to use our free will in the best way possible, thereby minimizing bad choices that we make, we must know what love is all about. To know what love is all about, we must know God, and to know God, we must spend some time with Him. We must set aside time each and every day for prayer and meditation. We must study the Gospels to learn about God's love, and we must practice what we learn through our service to others.

LUKE 22:54-65

Falling Down, Getting Up
(Matt. 26:57-58, 67-75. Mark 14:53-54, 66-72. John 18:12-18, 25-27)

Jesus has been arrested in the garden of Gethsemane and taken to the house of the high priest. He will wait there under guard for the council to question him early the next morning. While the guards made fun of him and beat him, people gathered in the nearby courtyard of the house, warming themselves against the night air with a small fire.

Peter is among them, in a delicate balance between wanting to stay near to his master and fleeing the impending danger. He feels safe as part of the group, until he is eventually recognized by a servant girl. "This man was with Jesus!" she exclaimed. His safety melted away with her words, and he was exposed to the danger.

Even though Peter was well-trained by Jesus, and presumably had a good understanding of Jesus's ministry and mission, the stress he was under created a fear that overpowered his spiritual core. He collapsed under its weight and his survival instinct kicked in, "Woman, I don't even know that man!" And it would happen again when someone else accused him, and it would happen yet one more time about an hour later, just as the rooster crowed.

The Lord, still nearby to Peter, turned to look at him. What was in his look? Disgust? Mercy? Compassion? Whatever it was, it made Peter remember that the Lord predicted that Peter would deny him three times before the rooster crowed. Peter had abandoned his true self. His failure was evident to him – it was a deep betrayal to his beliefs and his commitment to Jesus.

Anguish quickly flooded his mind, and he fled in a stream of bitter tears.

Peter was down, but was not lost. Over time he would regain his spiritual strength, grow from the experience of his failure, and play a prominent role in the formation and expansion of the early church.

Every one of us too, at one time or another, has experienced failure and disappointment in ourselves. Who hasn't experienced this? It's quite human, actually. That doesn't offer an excuse for past or future mishaps, but it does keep things in perspective.

To slip and fall as Peter did can happen whenever we're faced with a dark moment that's more powerful than our spiritual resources can bear. We're especially vulnerable when we don't have the presence of God in our hearts. Like Peter, we might have forgotten our spiritual moorings, our moral compass, or our heart connections. Something unexpected comes up (as it always seems to), and we're caught off guard. This can happen easily, especially in our highly sensory society where everything always moves at a fast pace no matter which way we look. Opportunities to pause and recharge our spiritual batteries are lacking because something else is demanding our time and attention.

The advice to "pray always" represents a way of life that can counterbalance the noise and pressures of the secular world. To pray always simply means to always have part of our attention and awareness on who and what we are in the eyes of God, never forgetting our purpose and meaning in life despite what other people demand from us or what they say about us.

This isn't easy to do, nor can we do it all the time. We are human, after all, and are subject to human instincts, desires and attachments. But the more we practice, the better we'll do in day-to-day events. We must take time to reclaim our soul, discovering who we truly are and what we're really supposed to be doing in this world. We can help find our true self through daily prayer, reflective study, and service to others – three paths that lead to a single unity and harmony in life.

Peter grew from his mistakes and so can we, especially when we keep in mind that we are supported by a loving God who is merciful and compassionate.

LUKE 22:66-71

The Trial Begins
(Matt. 26:59-66. Mark 14:55-64. John 18:19-24)

Early in the morning Jesus was brought before the council of chief priests and scribes for questioning. Here stood Jesus, the captive of their devious plot, finally within their grasp. The council was beginning to feel threatened by this man who brought new ideas to the people, ideas that could bring the council's power structure to ruins.

What would happen to their hierarchy if people were treated equally? How would their authority be compromised if people actually believed that they had access to God, and they no longer had to come to the religious leaders? What change would equity bring to the local economy? There were too many unknowns, and the change was too much. How dare this man claim he had the authority of God when it belonged to the council leaders?

The individual egos of the chief priests and scribes found a common enemy in this man who stood before them.

Dysfunctional egos normally work alone, seeking their own power and position against all others. Overinflated egos only use collaboration when faced with a common enemy. Alliances are formed, but will dissolve once the threat has been removed.

This new collective ego was looking for justification for their actions. They wanted to further their case against Jesus so that they could send it to the Roman authorities for resolution. If the Romans disposed this man, they could both rid themselves of this pest and keep their hands clean of his blood. Perhaps the Romans would realize that as a Messiah, Jesus would also be a threat to Roman rule, and therefore be neutralized.

"Tell us, are you the Messiah?" they asked. Jesus replied, "If I said so, you wouldn't believe me." Dysfunctional egos, especially mob collectives, have very strong filters and will only hear what they want to hear. It is often useless to reason with them.

"Are you the Son of God, then?" they demanded. But Jesus would only answer, "You say that I am." The collective quickly took this as an admission of Jesus's blasphemy, a confirmation of his insolence. "We need no more witnesses against this man!" they declared.

Jesus, seemingly powerless in the moment against this mindlessness, nevertheless proclaimed Divine victory: "But from now on the Son of Man will be seated at the right hand of the power of God." Evil may prevail in the moment, but it will never alter God's overall plan.

Free will choices, whether individual or as a group, may cause harm and damage – but God works around this, bringing Light to the Dark in many ways. God often intervenes in whatever way possible around each free will choice – before it happens, while it's happening, and after it happens by:

- altering events to influence the decision before it happens (for example, awakening our conscience, or providing a good value set to live by through prophets and teachers)
- providing support to those who *are being* adversely impacted by the decision (for example, as Jesus struggled with the agony of his impending ordeal, God sent an angel to Jesus to strengthen him)
- providing support to those who *have been* adversely impacted by the decision (for example, sending the Holy Spirit to teach, guide, and empower; building Church groups and communities that support each other).

If we can remember, as Jesus did, that God will eventually have His way and all will be well, we can muster the strength and support we need to get through the bleaker times. Jesus was to have a very rough day ahead of him, but the eventual outcome would seal God's love for people for all time and forever more.

LUKE 23:1-25

He Stirs Up the People
(Matt. 27: 1-2, 11-26. Mark 15:1-15. John 18:28-19:16)

Shortly after his arrest, Jesus was brought to Pilate by members of the council. The council hoped that Pilate would now find Jesus a threat to society and eliminate him. They pushed Jesus into Pilate's presence and began to accuse Jesus falsely. "He's perverting our nation!" some shouted. "He forbids us to pay tribute to Caesar!" yelled others. But none of the charges were true.

Pilate considered the matter and explained that he didn't believe that Jesus committed any crimes. "I find no crime in this man," Pilate concluded.

But the crowd was roused against Jesus, and they continued with their complaints. "He stirs up the people," they charged, "teaching his way throughout the land, from Galilee to here!"

When he heard this, Pilate saw a way to avoid the issue because if Jesus was a Galilean then he should actually be sent to Herod for trial. But Herod could find no fault with Jesus either, so he sent Jesus back to Pilate again. Several more times Pilate explained to the crowd that he could find no fault with Jesus, and tried to have him released. But under pressure from the crowd, he relented, and eventually allowed Jesus's execution.

The charge that Jesus "stirred up the people" was true. His message of love and wisdom fanned the embers burning within every human heart. The soul desires a connection with God and with those who know God. The richness of life comes when we can speak heart-to-heart with another person linked into the love of God.

We instinctively know when we're hearing the truth, and there often isn't enough of it to hear in this life. So when we do hear it, it's like a refreshing breeze or a cool drink on a hot day. We want more. Our hearts are stirred up and we must do something about it. That's how the people of Jesus's day felt, and it's how we feel today.

Certainly it would be better for those in positions of power and authority to have the common people kept quietly in their place. Things work much better for leaders if the masses are simply obedient and learn to accept what they get. But when things get too polarized, when some people have much more than others and some people begin to suffer beyond reason, it doesn't take much to stir them up.

The collective egos of the day did all they could to quiet this new revolutionary, Jesus. But he wouldn't stop; he wouldn't go away. So, in their last desperate act, they pressured the Roman authorities to eliminate Jesus.

LUKE 23:26-43

The Reign of Christ
(Matt. 27:31-44. Mark 15:21-32. John 19:17-27)

The last Sunday of the Church's liturgical cycle presents us with a rather surprising image – Jesus crucified on a cross between two other condemned men. This Sunday is often referred to as "the Reign of Christ." What we expect about our King is someone sitting victoriously on a high throne, ruling the world in all glory and power. Instead, we see what appears to be a broken man, suspended between two others who can't agree about who this person between them is.

Why are we presented with this image from the Passion experience as the culminating lesson after a year of lessons? Perhaps the explanation can be found not on a throne in some faraway kingdom, but at the core of every human heart.

Let's remember the key messages from many of the previous Gospel lessons: God is love itself; God dearly loves us; God came to earth through Christ to show us what He is like, and to teach us how to live; God wants us to love, too, and have a personal relationship with Him.

Internally, we are pressured by our survival and procreation instincts; because we are human flesh, we seek safety and comfort, we want security and power, and we want to experience the pleasures this world has to offer. These things are not evil, they are part of who we are as flesh and bones.

It's how we manage them that can create or prevent problems, which is often greatly influenced by *external* forces. We are shaped by the norms of our culture, marketing propaganda, peer pressure, social illusions, and past personal experience – all of which may press against our spiritual values, morals, and the conscience of our God-given soul.

The soul part of us often struggles with the worldly part of us. This is a battle we fight all of our lives. It's what makes us human, and what helps us to grow as children of God, especially when we deal with this tension in a proper way.

The two condemned men hanging on the opposite sides of Jesus represent the two sides of this battle. One of them joined in what the crowd was saying: "If you are the Messiah, save yourself! If you are the King, save yourself!" And they mocked and scoffed at Jesus. Our false self can easily accuse, reject, deny and disconnect from the truth. It's our worldly side getting the better of us, covering up our true self and our true identity – creating a world of darkness.

The other man represents our soul side. This man could see deeply, he could see the truth, and he was humble. Full of openness, understanding, and compassion, he surrendered himself to Jesus: "Remember me when you come into your kingdom." As Paul wrote in Col. 1:13, "He has rescued us from the power of darkness and transferred us in to the kingdom of His beloved Son..."

And there, in the middle of this personal struggle inside each of us, is Christ. Arms outstretched to bring the two sides together; he is always present between the tension of our worldly self and our true self. He is the mediator that knows and understands what we face as humans. He is the instrument of God to heal us, to bring us peace, to make us whole. Not there to accuse, condemn or punish, but ever-present to unite, redeem, and refresh.

Christ rules within our very heart. Christ stands amid our troubles and personal sorrows, mending and resting, healing and soothing.

The psalmist writes, "God is our refuge and strength, a very present help in trouble. Therefore we will not fear, though the earth itself should change, though the mountains shake in the heart of the sea ... The Lord of Hosts is with us ... Be still and know that I am God." (Ps. 46:10)

LUKE 23:44-49

The Death of Jesus
(Matt. 27:45-56. Mark 15:33-41. John 19:28-30)

Sometimes we can't see the enormity of our actions until they are completed. When Jesus took his last breath, the centurion suddenly realized that the man he helped execute was, in fact, innocent. It wasn't until the multitudes actually saw the broken body of Jesus on the cross that the horror of the crucifixion finally woke them up.

They realized the depths to which they sunk as part of the collective ego, the maddened mob that demanded the execution. And now the deed was done, and all they could do was beat their breasts in mental torment now plaguing their souls.

The broken Jesus hanging from the cross would become the universal Christian symbol of what mankind was capable of doing with an unfettered mind. It wasn't the Jews or the Romans that killed him, but the collective dysfunctional ego of those who surrendered their soul to the gods of the ages: power, position, wealth, prejudice and fear.

The crucified Christ is a reminder of how far humanity will go to pursue egoic desires and what it will do to defend them. Even the killing of the Son of God is not too much!

The image of the crucified Christ will hopefully serve as a reflective mirror for mankind. Perhaps it will shake us into reality and awaken us from an unconscious sleep before we act again. It can serve as a guidepost; a salvific tool if we gaze upon it and use it to remind us to take time to think about what we do or say before we do it or say it. What is the impact on ourselves and others if I think, do, or say this thing? Is it loving?

In this sense, Jesus's death *is* a key to salvation. The sacrifice wasn't as much an atonement for the world's sins, but more a reminder to keep us from making serious mistakes in our lives. A reminder of what can happen without God in our hearts. A reminder to turn to the wisdom of Jesus, providing us a path to reclaim our soul.

An equally important sacrifice was his *life*. Putting all other possibilities and opportunities aside, Jesus dedicated his entire life to teaching, healing, and showing us *how* to live together in peace and harmony. This was the wisdom that he shared with us. Nothing would get in his way to keep us from receiving this message of love, *even if it meant his own death* – which it ultimately did.

Continually, moment by moment, we must ask ourselves, "What one little thing can I do or say in this present moment to make it better?" The accumulation of all these improved present moments will lead to a much better life, and a much better world. The future is shaped by this little moment, right now.

LUKE 23:50-56

Love At What Cost?
(Matt. 27:57-61. Mark 15:42-47. John 19:38-42)

Joseph of Arimathaea, a member of the High Council, a good and righteous man, sat in the meeting where the plot against Jesus slowly grew. There was hatred in the air, floating on the currents of fear. Joseph sat there disagreeing with the proceedings, and yet remained quiet. How hard was it for him to be a part of something he found wrong, and yet not speak out against it?

John's Gospel indicates that Joseph kept his devotion to Jesus a secret because he was afraid of the repercussions that would follow. Perhaps he weighed the loss of his position and the power he enjoyed. What did he feel like at the critical moment when his voice was needed, and yet not heard? The tension within his soul must have been almost unbearable.

Would his voice, his one vote, have changed history? Would the Council have decided not to continue with their devious plan? We may never know.

Sometimes we find ourselves in a place where we wonder whether or not our vote, or our voice, would make any difference. "Does it really matter?" we may wonder. Then, deciding against speaking out, we rationalize it away, and let matters take their own course.

At other times, the anger within our soul is so strong that there is nothing to keep us silent, at any cost! We see an injustice, an abuse, some heinous act that demands an immediate response. We know that we just could not live with ourselves because the consequences of not responding, even if we are unsuccessful in our attempt to intervene, are too great.

Some battles are simply not worth the effort to fight. They are too small or insignificant to bother with. It may be that time will take care of it on its own. Sometimes the best decision is to do nothing at all.

In the monastic world, when someone wants to begin their spiritual journey within the Community, they are asked, "What are you saying 'Yes' to?" In other words, what is it that you're after? Certainly there is some gain to be had, or the choice wouldn't even be considered. But with each decision there comes a cost. So, the reverse side of this question is "What are you saying 'No' to?" What are you giving up? What's it going to cost you in terms of friends, career, luxuries, and benefits? What is the price you will pay for following this path of faith? It might not be cheap.

The cost was too high for Joseph of Arimathaea. But he didn't let go of his faith or his love even though he might have failed the moment. Joseph went and retrieved the body of Christ and prepared it for burial. He did what he could with what he had and who he was.

We journey along the path through life gradually becoming stronger in our convictions and knowledge of God's love for us. We pray that the challenges that confront us in life will come at a time when we are strong enough to bear them, or to at least bear them with others of like mind. Often, however, we seem to be alone in our struggle – but we must remember that we are never alone. The spirit and love of Christ is always with us, as it was with Joseph.

As we get to know Jesus and his love, we gradually devalue the things on which we used to put a high price, and we increase the value of those things He offers us: peace, joy, happiness, patience, kindness, gentleness, and wisdom.

LUKE 24:1-12

He Has Risen
(Matt. 28:1-10. Mark 16:1-8. John 20:1-10)

It was the first day of the week, at early dawn when the sun once again began to shed its light upon this land. The women who had followed Jesus all the way from Galilee returned to his tomb, bringing with them the spices that they had prepared for his body. When they arrived they found the stone had been rolled away from the tomb, so they went in. They found an empty tomb – Jesus was no longer there. His body was gone.

But what if instead they *had* found him still lying there. What if there had been no resurrection?

If there had been no resurrection, the women would have completed preparing Jesus's body and then returned to their homes. The disciples would gather together a few more times to discuss their recent experiences, wonder about what to do next, and perhaps gradually return to their old jobs. Would they have continued their mission? Would they have rallied at the death of Jesus and ventured out to foreign lands to spread the good news of Jesus? Would they have wondered whether this man was really a Son of God or just another human prophet? Would the message of God gradually fade under the weight of life's day-to-day challenges? What proof did they have to offer that this Jesus was, in fact, sent from God and that his message was the Word of God?

The resurrection of Jesus was perhaps the critical capstone covering the entire ministry of Jesus, and is the cornerstone of the Christian faith today. If the reports of his resurrection were fake, and he did not make additional appearances to hundreds of people after that first Easter, if Jesus did not become the

Christ, then the entire incredible history of this man from God would only claim a small part of the mythical genre of classical literature.

But the reports of Jesus's death were greatly exaggerated. The women entering the tomb found only the linens which covered Jesus's body. Two men, presumably angelic beings, reported that "He is risen." Jesus would not be found among the dead, because he was alive. Death could not contain him.

The resurrection of Jesus was God's great statement to mankind that Jesus was undeniably sent by Him to Earth to heal us, to teach us, and to show us how to live together as Children of God. In spite of the collective egos of the time banding together to publicly execute this divine messenger, God's plan would not be compromised! The resurrection of Jesus was God's proof that nothing can come between Him and His love for us – even the murder of His own Son.

The resurrection was God's way of proving that the message was true, Jesus was true, and His love was true. God's love for us is unconditional, and unending. The path to God was now freely open, and the perpetual invitation extended to everyone. Jesus, the man, was now Christ, the Advocate and sustainer.

The Christmas gift to us of this Son of Man was validated through the Easter Resurrection. He is ours, and we are His.

LUKE 24:13-35

To Emmaus and Back Again
(Mark 16:12, 13)

Two of Jesus's followers finally left Jerusalem and headed back to Emmaus, their village a short distance away. It was a couple of days after the crucifixion, and they were among many who weren't quite sure what to do. They had hoped that Jesus was the one who would redeem Israel, but now these hopes had been dashed at the foot of the cross.

They were in an uncomfortable situation, and had only a few choices. Like many situations we find ourselves in, we can:

- **change** the situation we're in
- **leave** the situation we're in
- **accept** the situation we're in.

If we don't do one of these three, then we induce suffering upon ourselves. When this suffering happens, we begin to hear ourselves complaining, we might feel fear or irritation, we might get confused or feel discontent. We can become miserable to be around.

Cleopas and his traveling partner decided to leave the situation that they were in and go back home to Emmaus. But they still felt empty inside because they carried with them some deep disappointments from their recent past. They couldn't "let go of it." They couldn't change what had happened, but they couldn't accept it either. So, on the road to Emmaus, they talked it over, and tried to make some sense of it.

That's when the stranger appeared – someone who would help them to see the truth of the matter. The stranger was the risen Jesus. But they didn't recognize Jesus at first. Why?

Because they were so wrapped up in their own helplessness that it was blinding them from understanding, from "seeing."

In this passage of Luke, Jesus first appealed to their reason. "Beginning with Moses and the prophets, he interpreted to them the things about himself in all the scriptures." But their minds were too busy dealing with confusion, denial, rationalization, and pity. They still could not see Jesus.

So, Jesus then went straight for their hearts, past the logic of the mind, past reasoning that often darkens the imagination of the spirit, past the stumbling blocks of objections and memories, and straight to the home of the soul.

He sat down with them at a table of gathering, a place where heart can be with heart, and he broke bread with them. This meal pushed aside all the raging thoughts in their minds about the past and the future, and brought them into the present moment where love abounds. The bread of life from the hand of God is a symbol of unity, peace, and presence.

This Eucharistic act pushes back the past, and delays the future, leaving only the precious present moment. It's only *in this very moment*, right now, that the pathways to God are opened, and the Light of His love will shine in. It's the only place of peace, because there is none offered by the past, and none revealed by the future.

The Bread of Life is here and now, and this brought instant recognition to the two travelers. It was Jesus here with us, in our hearts all the time! "Were not our hearts burning with joy within us while he was talking to us on the road?" This was indeed the risen Christ!

The empty tomb means that Jesus left the physical world and is now present everywhere in the spiritual world, which includes the very home of our soul. Immanuel – God is indeed with us! The Christmas Gift to us is completed in the Resurrection.

Jesus gave the two travelers a new perspective which turned their gloom and doom into deep joy. Unable to contain their excitement, they returned to Jerusalem that very evening to share their story.

LUKE 24:36-49

The Appearance
(Matt. 28:16-20. Mark 16:14-18. John 20:19-23)

The remaining eleven disciples and some of their companions were huddled together in a safe place after what they perceived was a disastrous weekend. They were sharing their stories, trying to comfort one another, when Jesus appeared among them and said, "Peace be with you!" In their state of mind, they thought they were seeing a ghost.

Trying to calm them, Jesus showed them the wounds on his hands and feet, telling them to touch him. "See? A ghost has no flesh and bones as you can see that I have." As further proof he ate a piece of fish in front of them.

As they began to understand and believe, Jesus affirmed what was written in the scriptures about him, and what he said would happen to him has indeed happened! Their confusion and fear turned to joy, washing away the doubts that plagued them since the crucifixion. All that Jesus taught them was true! He was sent from God to heal, and to teach, and to show how to make the most of this earthly life in honor of God.

They had been taught by Jesus that God is merciful, compassionate, and loving. If Jesus hadn't been resurrected, these truths may have faded under the pressures of daily life and persecution by the authorities. But it *was* true! All that he said and did came from God Himself!

The disciples now had new energy and a renewed purpose. The truth revitalized their belief, as well as their desire to continue their mission. But the disciples and their companions still needed the presence of the Holy Spirit, soon to be sent to them. So they were asked to stay in the city until they received this power from on high.

Those present at this appearance saw that the wounds of Jesus were still evident on his body. Perhaps they wondered why these weren't healed at the resurrection. I suspect Jesus carried these wounds to remind us that even though the lowest depths of mankind could harm the son of God, the highest love of God for them could not be compromised. The wounds of Jesus had not healed because the world itself was not yet healed. Perhaps when the world finally heals, these wounds, too, will be gone.

Jesus was rejected, but very forgiving. This is the way of God. The path to eternal wholeness doesn't start with punishment, but forgiveness. Often repentance follows forgiveness – a new life is built when it sees that there is a way to wholeness. It is planted and nurtured with mercy and compassion, watered with tears of joy.

One day all souls will be brought back home into the arms of God. For some the journey will be short and fast. Others will resist and gnash their teeth. But the loving patience and care of God through His Son will eventually be enough to win them over. No soul will be left behind.

LUKE 24:50-53

From Jesus to Christ
(Mark 16:19-20)

As Jesus parts company from his disciples, ascending into heaven, it seems as though his earthly presence is over. But, of course, it's not over – it's just beginning.

Jesus, now as the Christ, is an eternal power once again that can reach everyone. Truly, he now abides in us and we in him. Through him, we can reach across the ages and realms through the warmth of our hearts, to be with him and he with us.

As Paul wrote in his letter to the Ephesians, "God put this power to work in Christ when He raised him from the dead and seated him at His right hand in the heavenly places, far above all rule and authority and power and dominion, and above every name that is named, not only in this age but also in the age to come." (Eph. 1:20-21)

The proof of God's love for us was demonstrated in the Resurrection and Ascension of Jesus. Even though the collective ego of mankind rejected Jesus's message of love and peace, brutally murdering him, God would prove that Jesus was indeed sent by Him, and that Jesus's message was true and good. God's love for us is steadfast and endures forever. He is ready to help each of us reclaim our soul, and to become what we were meant to be.

Bringing it All Together

So, what does this all mean? How can a person put this information to good use? How can it change my life for the better? Where do I start?

We'd all like a better world, and we'd like it right away. But things just don't happen that way. Since the world is the sum total of all the individuals who live here, the only way to make a better world is to begin with oneself. If people could discover who they really are, to really know who they are and what they're supposed to be doing in their lives, then the world itself would begin to change for the better.

Ultimately, this translates into a goal to know, love and serve the Lord in our own unique way, using the gifts, talents and interests we have been given. It involves seeking out and reclaiming our true soul from beneath the burden of social norms, expectations and pressures. It means being honest with ourselves, and shedding the values that society places on us if they do not resonate with our soul. It means facing our shadow side and integrating it into our consciousness, allowing us to become complete human beings.

We are spiritual beings having a physical experience. The spiritual piece of us is eternal, but the physical side is subject to all the laws of nature. There is a natural tension between survival and individuation. But this tension creates movement, and drives us toward self-fulfillment.

Let's look at each of the steps from the inside out.

Nurturing Our Soul

It all begins with our core, our soul. If we don't have the right tools, equipment, and attitude, we won't be much help to anyone else. So, the place to begin is with ourselves. No one is perfect, of course, and we needn't wait until we think we are perfect before extending a helping hand. Often we improve ourselves by helping others, so part of nurturing our own soul is to help other people nurture theirs. It's an issue of balance – reaching out to others to the extent that we can, and in some way help someone else. As we grow, so will our ability to help others. So don't hesitate to share a smile, offer a blessing, or lend an ear to someone who needs to be heard. Little things matter!

Some of the basic self-nurturing tools and tips we can use are found in the Gospels. We listen to the wisdom of Jesus, and we watch how he lived his life. What can be gleaned from our Gospel journey?

- Prayer: Jesus spent a lot of time in prayer. Prayer is spending time alone with God, listening and expressing our soul-based desires and offering prayers for others. Prayer *does* change things – mostly ourselves – and that's how bigger change happens. There are different prayer forms that can be used depending on our temperaments. Some people just sit silently in a sacred space. Others will take walks in nature as their prayer time. Some people meditate; others sing! Whatever brings us closer to the Presence of God is good.
- Worship: This is a group form of prayer. It, too, can bring us closer to the Presence of God, but it also lets us know that there are other people on the journey, too.

It's very helpful to know that there are other like-minded people that are seeking this personal growth. The trappings of a church service can create the proper mindset for us to be open to God's guidance and comfort.

- Study: Our "Owner's Manual," if you will, includes the Gospels. Jesus knew the Hebrew scriptures very well. The Gospels should always be a part of our weekly, if not daily, study. But there are lots of other things to learn, too. The more we know about people and about the world, the more we are likely to change life for the better. We can study and sharpen our skills in whatever truly interests us, because all these things can be used by God at the right time and place. Somehow, we are all part of the overall plan of interconnection, and contribute to the greater good. We don't have to save a nation or cure a disease to be in God's favor. He appreciates even a smile or helping hand to someone else.
- Support team: Jesus had twelve disciples and a number of other people who stayed with him on his journey. It's very helpful to have a small team of trusted people walk with us on our journey. Consider working with a spiritual director, counselor, therapist, physician, or close friends on a regular basis. These should not be people who want to make us more like themselves, but people who can help us to discover our true selves. They may have to challenge us to do so.
- Present Moment Awareness: Jesus knew what was going on around him. He even felt the needful touch on the hem of his garment while walking through a crowd. He noticed things because he took the time to do so. We

often move too fast through life, missing the little gifts and abundant blessings that are scattered in our path. We need to take time to see, really see what's in front of us. We must listen to the sounds that we normally block out. We need to feel the textures and surfaces of the things we touch. We should walk through each moment of the day at half-speed to get the full richness it has to offer. Practice the Presence of God around us. He's everywhere!

- Celebrate! Jesus celebrated many events. Let us celebrate birthdays, weddings, anniversaries, confirmations, graduations, holidays, and births. St. Paul wrote that when one of us is honored, we are all honored. Celebrations are shared events that remind us we are all an interconnected family of the children of God.

So there's a place to start. There are probably other ways to nurture the soul, some which work well for you. Take care of your inner-most being. And as you do that, also being to think about the place where your soul resides – your body.

Nurturing the House of Our Soul: Our Bodies

We have been given a temporary house for our souls. Some day we have to return it to its Creator. In the meantime, the better we take care of it, the better able we will be to nurture our souls and serve others in this world.

Knowing what's right to do for our bodies is not easy. It seems as though every week the recommended dietary guidelines are changing, sometimes to the exact opposite of what they were a short time ago. Marketing doesn't help much either, because there are companies out there whose primary interest is profit, and not your health. As a result, navigating through the world of nutrition and medicine is dangerous at best. As mankind becomes more "advanced," so do medical and mental health maladies. It seems as though the wealthiest nations are also the sickest.

So, despite all the "well-intended" advice about what to do for optimum health, we must think for ourselves. Common sense plays a role here, as does what actually works for you. And, we must remember, due to the complex nature of the human body, what works for one person may not work well for another. So, share your discoveries, but be careful about insisting that your way is the magic bullet we've all been looking for. I have been using a high *natural* fat, low-carbohydrate diet for years quite successfully, but it may not work well for others. (For me, natural fat does not include partially hydrogenated oils, vegetable oils, or margarine!)

Does exercise matter? Yes, but again, some people like to knock themselves out running marathons, while others (like myself) believe that working in a garden is sufficient. The body was designed to move around, so, if you can, move it! But do it in a way that you enjoy and fits your routine.

God thought that rest was important enough for us humans that He made a commandment to take one day a week off. It's called the Sabbath. It may be the most neglected commandment He's given us (well, perhaps having other gods instead of Him might rank higher in neglect). Rest is part of the natural work-rest cycle that we can't ignore without a cost. Many people are sleep-deprived getting worn out by a fast-paced life. Busy schedules may prevent much needed rest during the week, but we could all try to do a better job of rest on that precious seventh day.

Your soul lives in your body, and your body lives in your home. Let's spend a little time now on that.

Nurturing the House of Our Body: Our Home

Home is what we make it and where we make it. In this country, some people have more homes than they can remember, and for others it may be just a park bench. This inequity is a serious issue, and a very shameful one. I believe that this situation will gradually change for the better when more people nurture their own souls. Those people with too much will be willing to share, and better opportunities will be made for those less fortunate so that they can obtain their own homes.

But wherever we call home, it should be considered a sacred space whether we own, rent, or are a guest somewhere. Our home space is our personal monastery, and should be treated as such. Ideally, our home space is sufficient for our true needs, and is manageable within our means. Our home and related personal property exist to serve us, and we should not be imprisoned by it. As our servant, our home is to be cared for and treated with respect. Keep things well-maintained. When we no longer need some of our stuff, share it – give it away, sell it, or recycle it. Leave as small an imprint upon this earth as possible; replenish the earth, Genesis says – we have nowhere else to go!

A good monastery dedicates spaces for specific things. For example, there is a special place for prayer. It may be a corner of a bedroom, or in a spare room. It may be a special place in the yard, or at a local park. Try to avoid using this space for anything but prayer. There is a special place for sleeping, and a special place for study, too. Keep it simple!

Nurturing the House of Our Home: Our World

As all these things come together, there will be a positive impact on those around us – not only our immediate neighbors, but on our community, our cities, our nation, and the world. Remember that groups of people, no matter how large, are made up of individuals. Change the individuals, and you change the group. It needs to be done one person at a time, beginning with you.

To serve the Lord is to glorify Him through you. And the best way to do that is to become who you were truly meant to be. Sometimes we spend most of our life trying to figure this out. That's quite understandable considering the shaping and molding that goes on as we grow up and try to find our way through life. Society wants us to shape us into one thing, our parents sometimes want to shape us into another, or our friends have their own ideas, too. Certainly pointing out the good and bad things in life is fine – but when all this shaping runs counter to our true selves we end up getting lost.

We often heard as we grew up, "You can be anything you want to be. Just put your mind to it!" Eventually we learn, however, that the only thing we can truly be is what we were made to be. There is precious little help in discovering this, so we often don't get a chance to explore it until we are much older. But hopefully we figure it out, finally realizing what's important in life, and begin to reclaim our soul.

I pray that this book has been at least a small help in the process.

Reclaiming Your Soul

TOPICAL INDEX

Topic	Page
Abundance	62, 122, 128, 145, 161, 171, 205
Abuse	11, 36, 90, 160, 166, 170, 193, 197, 236
Acceptance	76, 112, 190, 200, 210
Achievement	97, 148
Action	44, 70, 73, 74, 85, 95, 109, 110, 112, 141, 155, 159, 181, 234
Activity / Busy-ness	41, 65, 73, 84, 107, 114, 124, 137, 138, 194, 211, 241, 249
Attachments	20, 23, 25, 36-38, 128, 129, 148, 150, 152, 165, 180, 181, 198, 211, 214, 226
Attitude	190, 246
Awakening	38, 65, 68, 69, 91, 92, 103, 113, 149, 157, 160, 162, 164, 165, 172, 184, 200, 214, 215, 221, 229, 234
Awareness (Mindfulness)	10, 25, 35, 38, 40, 44, 56, 62, 66, 67, 71-73, 76, 86, 101, 103, 105, 109, 118, 128, 129, 140, 147, 162, 171, 176, 178, 179, 184, 186, 200, 203, 214, 221, 226, 247
Balance in Life	52, 58, 65, 75, 95, 102, 109, 124, 131, 167, 171, 174, 200, 225, 246
Baptism	24, 25, 47, 195, 196

Being Human	95, 97, 122, 147, 149, 168, 179, 194, 214, 225, 231
Benedictus	7-9, 20
Burdens	22, 68, 97, 99, 121, 147, 150, 157, 159, 167, 220, 245
Care-giving	13, 28, 36, 117, 125, 243, 248
Children	4, 9, 11, 15, 16, 19, 23, 53, 54, 64, 73, 89, 99, 103, 105, 111, 120, 132-134, 138, 147-149, 151, 159, 160, 170, 174, 177-179, 198, 201, 202, 206, 217, 232, 239, 248
Collaboration	47, 76, 161, 228
Confession	156, 194
Connectedness	(see Interconnectedness)
Consciousness	(see Awakening)
Contemplation	8, 109, 110, 115, 124, 200
Corruption	8, 61
Cost of Discipleship	102, 150, 155, 169, 177, 235-237
Dangers of Being Christian	16, 28, 48, 52, 63, 97, 132, 204, 207, 212
Day of Judgment	22, 25, 71, 72, 134, 155
Decision Making	31, 39, 54-56, 62, 64, 145, 149, 155, 198, 224, 236
Demons	37, 40, 82, 83, 96, 102, 115, 203
Dignity	10, 32, 47, 89
Discernment	28, 54-56, 65, 107, 119, 127

Economics	17, 32, 48, 53-57, 64, 65, 89, 98, 123-126, 132, 145, 154, 161-166, 201, 207
Ego, Dysfunctional	8, 17, 25, 32, 36-40, 47, 49, 53, 64-68, 76, 83, 87, 89, 90, 96, 100, 102, 103, 105, 106, 113-116, 118-120, 128, 130, 135, 143, 148, 161-165, 171-172, 180, 183, 192-199, 203-208, 212-215, 218, 221-222, 227-228, 231, 234, 239, 244
Emotion	1, 20, 43, 53, 128-129, 150, 170
Enemies	7-8, 20-21, 60, 99, 103, 145-146, 150, 211-212, 227
Enlightenment	16, 35, 50, 72, 78, 118, 140, 165
Eternal Life	1, 12, 13, 22, 106, 127-128, 134, 152, 180-182, 219, 221, 243-245
Eucharist	91-93, 216, 241
Faith	17:1-10; 8:22-25; 22:31-38
Failure	219, 225-226
False Self	6, 13, 37, 89, 120-121, 140, 143, 150, 161-162, 175-177, 184, 187, 192, 196, 198, 203, 204, 232
Family of God	13, 16, 17, 24, 28, 30, 33, 79, 91-93, 104, 110-111, 128, 132, 165, 169, 176, 202, 206, 209, 248

Fear 1-2, 7-9, 15, 20, 23, 30, 37, 40, 43,
47, 53, 57, 64, 68, 76, 80-81, 84, 95,
107-108, 120-121, 128, 132, 145,
148, 153-154, 159, 163, 165-166,
175, 178, 181, 192, 198, 211, 217,
225, 233-235, 240, 242

Forgiveness 44-45, 63, 74, 112, 122, 131, 138,
157-159, 221, 243

Foundations, Spiritual 63, 66, 134, 149

Free Will 55, 61, 64, 76, 82, 100, 114, 121,
143, 207, 221-224, 228

Frustrations 77, 84, 95, 97, 170

Glorifying God 149-152

Greatness 97, 218

Greed 8, 20, 23, 61, 114, 119, 122-124,
143, 163-164, 173, 192, 198, 204,
211

Hospitality 109, 201-202

Human Being .... (see Being Human)

Humility 34, 67, 87-89, 146-147, 179,
191-192

Hypocrisy 118, 120-122, 203-204

Identity 14, 27, 30, 52, 59, 67, 83, 100, 114,
172, 175-177, 189, 233

Incarnation 12, 21, 203, 210, 221

Independence 102-103

Instincts 99, 145, 148, 218, 225-227, 231-232

Interconnectedness	5, 11, 13, 28, 35, 37-38, 44, 46, 48, 54, 65, 71, 88, 92, 99-100, 104-105, 108, 111, 114, 120, 122, 127-129, 138, 140, 145, 157-158, 161, 164, 170, 173-178, 192, 200, 206, 209, 220-221, 224, 226, 230, 247-248
Interruptions	84-86, 185
Joy	4, 5, 8, 9, 13, 16, 17, 19, 21, 25, 31, 68, 100-104, 121, 132, 155, 161, 179, 181, 212, 216-217, 237, 241-243
Judgment	21, 71, 155, 162, 189
Justice	10, 56, 58, 69-72, 130, 134-135, 141-142, 155-156, 173-174, 198, 210, 222, 236
Kingdom of God	3-5, 10, 16, 25, 34, 52, 57, 58, 76, 77, 91, 97, 98, 102, 103, 111, 112, 118, 121, 122, 124, 125-131, 139-143, 147-149, 160-164, 169-172, 178-182, 191, 197-202, 207-209, 214, 218, 232-233
Leadership	17, 48, 49, 66, 81, 118-119, 183, 195, 213, 218, 231
Life after Death	(see Eternal Life)
Light	8, 16, 21, 37, 78-79, 117-118, 162, 164, 175, 184, 186, 203, 228, 241
Lord's Prayer	58, 76, 111, 169, 200, 202

Love	1-2, 11, 13, 15, 32, 52, 55, 61, 96, 112, 121-122, 124, 130, 134, 140, 145-146, 151, 153-161, 165, 167, 181, 183, 186, 190, 196, 206, 209, 214, 216-217, 221, 223, 224, 230, 241, 245
Love, four degrees	168-170
Love of God	3, 4, 6, 7, 9, 12, 16, 18, 21-23, 25, 29, 30, 33-35, 41, 54-55, 61, 63-65, 68, 69, 71, 75, 78-79, 83, 94, 100-101, 103, 105, 110, 112-116, 119, 125, 127-128, 131, 133, 135-136, 138, 139, 144, 147, 149, 152, 154-155, 160, 162, 166, 172-174, 176, 184, 186-188, 191-195, 198-199, 203, 206-212, 221, 223, 229, 232, 235, 237, 239, 243-244
Love our Neighbor	47, 49, 53, 59-60, 72-74, 89-90, 92, 97-99, 102, 106, 133, 145, 151, 202
Magnificat, the	3, 5-6
Mankind's Way	50-51, 66-67, 122-124, 144-146, 158-160, 172-172, 199-200
Marriage	201-202
Mental Health	20, 40, 43, 71, 82-84, 128-129, 204, 223, 234, 249
Mercy	3, 5, 7, 13, 20-21, 31, 42, 72, 95-96, 99, 102, 127, 136, 139, 143, 155,

	167, 183, 185, 187, 194, 199, 212, 222, 225, 243
Mind-Body Connections	43-45
Mission of Jesus	15, 20, 33, 46, 54, 85-87, 96-97, 119, 193, 214-215, 225, 238, 243
Money	(see Wealth)
Mountaintop Experience	95-97
Names	14, 28, 102
Nature	1, 14, 44, 75, 80, 88, 91-92, 114-115, 124, 133, 138, 144, 206, 245, 246
Nature of God	5, 7, 34, 47, 69, 105, 168
Peace	8, 12, 16, 20-22, 32, 45, 56, 68, 100-101, 121-122, 126, 129-133, 138, 140, 146, 152, 161, 171, 187, 207, 220, 233, 235, 237, 241-244
Perception	72-74, 173
Physical World	1, 13, 29, 31-33, 44-45, 49, 51-52, 68-69, 95-96, 99, 105, 123-124, 127-130, 145, 148, 152, 165, 168, 170, 172, 186, 241, 245
Planning	41, 55
Possessions (property)	35, 122-124, 128, 148, 150-152, 181
Power	2, 3, 6, 8-9, 12, 15, 17, 20, 23, 25, 29-38, 43, 48-49, 52, 57, 61, 64, 66-68, 72, 81, 83, 85, 87, 89-92,

                                        97-98, 102, 108, 110, 112, 114-117, 119, 121, 126, 140, 143, 160, 163, 171, 173-174, 178, 182-190, 193, 195, 203-218, 222-224, 227-228, 231-236, 243-244

Prayer 5, 7, 9, 20, 28, 54, 83, 89, 105, 109, 111-113, 115, 122, 124, 127, 131, 138, 151, 167, 173-174, 196, 200, 209, 211, 219, 224, 227, 246, 250

Prejudice 8, 17, 20, 23, 64, 68, 83, 121, 143, 148, 150, 175, 181, 192, 198, 211, 234

Presence of God 15, 16, 22-23, 35, 37, 62, 81, 83, 89, 94, 109-113, 115, 118, 131, 144, 188, 192, 197, 207, 212, 214, 217, 219, 222, 226, 243, 246, 248

Present Moment 5, 35, 41, 73, 84, 86, 95, 107, 118, 128, 130, 167, 188, 190, 235, 241, 247

Problem Solving 42-43, 240-242

Purpose of Christianity 56-60, 111-113

Purpose in Life 5-6, 12-13, 102-103, 187-188, 207-209

Reality 40, 48, 128, 177-179, 234

Relationships 7, 21, 30-31, 45, 71, 94, 106, 108, 111, 114, 128, 131, 149, 151, 157, 168, 180, 189, 195, 202, 210, 232

Religion 48, 91-93
Resistance 49, 67, 76, 162, 223
Resurrection 69, 90, 99, 116, 151, 184, 201,
                            238-239, 242-244
Sabbath 50-52, 137-139, 249
Salvation 3, 6, 8, 16, 21-23, 56, 94, 117, 119,
                            167, 184, 187-188, 215, 217, 235
Sensitivity 67, 74, 85-86, 180, 200
Service 36, 89, 102-103, 106, 109-110, 113,
                            115, 131, 140, 155, 167, 196, 218,
                            224, 227
Sin 22, 29, 44-46, 57-58, 74, 98, 112,
                            120-122, 155, 158, 178, 183, 215,
                            220-221, 235
Spiritual Direction Team 8, 97, 115, 211, 247
Study, Reflective 62, 89, 109, 113, 115, 122, 127, 131,
                            162, 167, 172, 224, 227, 247, 250
Suffering 30, 33, 45, 47, 53, 82-83, 124-125,
                            130, 147, 157, 161, 163, 165, 170,
                            208, 222, 231, 240
Talents 6, 59, 98, 101-103, 105, 108, 151,
                            158, 162, 175, 178, 182, 189-190,
                            196, 209, 245
Temple of God 18-19, 162, 169
Temptations 28-31, 102, 113, 199
Thinking 7, 10, 35, 39-41, 43, 51, 54, 59, 88,
                            91, 167, 172, 211, 234, 249

Term	Pages
Toleration	46-47
Transformation	24-25, 38, 56, 60-62, 112, 151, 198
True Self (Soul)	6, 13, 25, 37-38, 40-41, 47, 66-67, 83, 89, 103, 118-122, 129, 143, 148-149, 151-152, 161, 164-165, 172, 175-178, 183-184, 192, 196, 198, 203, 212, 214, 224-225, 227, 233, 247, 251
Trust	64, 123, 125-127, 179
Truth	25, 33, 35, 37, 40, 45, 50-51, 68, 91, 100, 104-105, 118, 121, 130, 155, 160, 162, 164, 172, 179, 184, 186, 188, 192-194, 196, 198, 204, 208, 231-233, 243
Unforgivable Sin	120-122
Unity	45, 49, 68, 70, 72, 89, 92, 104, 110, 111, 114, 122, 132, 136, 145-146, 160, 193, 206, 217, 227, 241
Vulnerability	1, 28, 44, 52-53, 61, 95, 148, 226
Wealth	6, 36, 57-58, 64, 121, 126, 149, 157-160, 163, 179-181, 183, 188, 208, 234, 249
Wisdom of Jesus	62, 126, 184, 214, 235, 246
Word of God	75-77, 79, 81, 117-118, 153, 238
Worthiness	38, 52, 66, 72-73, 94, 133, 148, 154, 166, 185, 214

About the Author

Daniel D. Schroeder completed his undergraduate studies in Classical Hebrew at the University of Wisconsin-Milwaukee. He is the founder of the Community of the Gospel, a dispersed monastic Episcopal Christian Community which has members across the United States. Daniel also has a Master of Science in adult educational psychology and an MBA in finance. He and his wife live in east central Wisconsin. Daniel can be reached at:

BeneVentura, LLC
PO Box 414
Hortonville, WI 54944

www.communityofthegospel.org

www.ingramcontent.com/pod-product-compliance
Lightning Source LLC
Chambersburg PA
CBHW032031290426
44110CB00012B/755